Maximize Your Personal Injury Settlement

MAXIMIZE YOUR PERSONAL INJURY SETTLEMENT

Fighting Insurance and the System

JACK FINE

Expert Press

Maximize Your Personal Injury Settlement
Fighting Insurance and the System

Jack J. Fine
Fine, Farkash, & Parlapiano, PA
622 NE 1st St
Gainesville, FL 32601
(352) 376-6046
www.ffplaw.com

ISBN-13: 978-1-946203-36-6

Contents

Introduction

IF YOU HAVE BEEN in an accident or been injured in some way, the prospect of pursuing a personal injury claim can be overwhelming and intimidating. For many people, the aftermath of an accident or injury is their first-ever encounter with a lawyer. The average person has no idea what a lawyer really does. They don't know how to pick an attorney, deal with an attorney, or discuss their case with an attorney. And they probably don't know that they can hire a personal injury lawyer without incurring huge legal bills, thanks to the contingency system.

If you're in that situation, it can feel like you're shooting in the dark.

With this book, I hope to take some of the mystery and the fear out of that process. I want to help people to understand how the process works, at least from the perspective of one lifelong plaintiff's lawyer.

I also hope to counter some of the negative misperceptions that our society holds about lawyers. I've heard all the stories and the lawyer jokes. And I know that much of that negative information gets spread by insurance companies and others in our society who have an agenda. It's an agenda that essentially puts profits over people.

Of course there are all different kinds of attorneys, and I certainly don't claim to speak for them all. I'm writing from my own perspective and my own decades of experience as a lawyer. My particular background includes criminal defense law as well as plaintiffs' personal injury law. I also have a background in teaching trial practice to law students.

In this book, I will share some of my own experience and offer information that I hope will help you in the event of accident or injury. I hope that you never find yourself in that situation, but life comes at us in unexpected ways. Let me help you respond to the unexpected.

Author's Note: I realize that not every reader will need to read through every chapter of this book. For a quick reference guide to auto accidents, see page 169.

Chapter 1: The Road to Gainesville

EVERY JOURNEY has a beginning. You may be starting your journey after being injured in an accident, and I hope that this book will be a great help to you. I've written this book because of the journey I've been on for over 35 years, helping people like you.

Regardless of the destination, a journey is always better when you have someone travelling with you. That's what we do with our clients, and that's how I ended up doing what I do to help people like you. Let me start by sharing with you a bit of my journey. And then, throughout the rest of this book, I'm going to offer information that may help you on your own journey.

I grew up in New Jersey, and graduated from high school in northern New Jersey, not far from New York. When I came to Florida, I was a recent graduate of a four-year liberal arts college. I had applied to the University of Florida because my parents were moving to Florida in their retirement. I thought it would be a good idea to go to school as an in-state resident.

I didn't know what I wanted to do after college, but I thought law school would be an interesting choice. Back then, we didn't have any lawyers in our family, but my brother had gone to law school and he was just finishing school.

We were the first generation in our family to get a college education. My parents always valued education very highly; my mother and my father sacrificed greatly to make it possible for their children not just to go to college, but to attend the college of their choice. Of course at that time, college wasn't as astronomically expensive as it is now.

My parents encouraged us to go to school and get a good education. I'm not sure I lived up to their goals because I wasn't the world's greatest student as an undergraduate. But I decided to work really hard in law school at the University of Florida. I didn't know what to expect.

I graduated college in May, but I wasn't starting law school until spring semester, so I had almost a full year off. I spent that time in a variety of jobs in south Florida, from working as a security guard, to doing construction work, to teaching tennis. By the time I started law school, I was pretty happy to get back to the academic routine as opposed to carrying block and rebar.

So after that year off I came to Gainesville, with my dog Mojo, a half St. Bernard, half Labrador Retriever. We rented a very small apartment and I would walk or bicycle to my law school classes.

At that time, there were two sections of 100 students each at the University of Florida College of Law. We had a set group of classes, which included the standard torts, contracts, constitutional law, and eventually criminal law. I got better grades in law school than I did as an undergraduate because I took it more seriously and worked much harder.

The law classes were taught with the Socratic method. That's a method of education that's unfamiliar to most people unless they've seen the old movie or TV series, *The Paper Chase*.

In the Socratic method, the law professor stands up and questions the students continuously about the readings, primarily cases that the students have prepared the night before. You answer the professor and he asks you more questions. At no time did the law professors ever tell you what the law is, or tell you how to be a lawyer, at least in your first or second years of law school.

That's a bit disconcerting, particularly when you have exams at the end of the semester. You've never done these essay-type exams before and your grade rests on one final exam. It's a somewhat nerve-wracking experience—it can be almost like a hazing, depending on the law professor.

I continued with these Socratic classes until I took a course called clinic or clinic preparation, which was a preparation for a clinical experience. The term clinic, when used in law school, means you go out to work for someone in the real world of the law. It's like an internship. I chose to work for the public defender's office. I had never even seen the inside of a law office before; I hadn't done clerking as many students do. This was at the end of my second year or the beginning of my third year of law school.

Honestly, I had no idea how it all worked. I had no idea that the paperwork is organized into files. This was before computers, so all the paperwork would go into a paper file. How it was all organized was a revelation to me—that's how naive I was. But I really liked the individual lawyers in the public defender's office. They were extremely dedicated. They appeared to be knowledgeable and competent. I looked up to them, particularly the lawyers who handled felonies because those were the most serious cases.

Under rules passed by the Supreme Court of the State of Florida, the clerks—or the interns, which is really what they were—would be allowed to do some actual work. If you were lucky, you got to do a trial. I would always volunteer for stuff, so I got to do not only some trial work but also an appeal. The trials would not be felonies; they would be misdemeanors or traffic cases, but I did get to do trial work.

I really enjoyed my time as a clerk in the public defender's office and I learned a lot there. The first thing I was asked to do in court was something called a change of plea. This is done when an individual is going to change their plea from not guilty to guilty. Once the individual pled guilty, the judge would sentence them to a particular sentence. Usually it was time served, by agreement with the state, and the individual would then get out of jail.

My supervising attorney said, "Jack, do you want to do this change of plea? Go see the client." He went with me into the holding cell to talk it over with the client who, although he was charged with a misdemeanor shoplifting, was a repetitive shoplifter. We went into the cell and explained it to the client. We told him, "Hey, you're going to change your plea. The maximum sentence is 60 days but you've already served six days in jail, so the odds are we'll just get you time served."

We went back out and I told the judge that we were ready to do the change of plea. The judge's name was Cathy Wright. She was quite brilliant, but also very stern. She brought in the defendant. Now when judges sentence people, they have to tell them what the maximum potential sentence is. Judge Wright said, "Mr. So and So, you understand that you're pleading guilty and the maximum possible sentence is 60 days." At that point, the defendant, my client, whom I had just met about ten minutes earlier, started screaming, "No, I don't want to change my plea; I can't have that sentence." It caused quite an uproar in the court. The judge gave me a disgusted look and said, "Mr. Fine, take your client back to the holding cell. We will not accept his plea at this point."

It was certainly an interesting experience for me. I was startled and upset, but my mentor, the supervising attorney, explained that these kinds of things happened. The client was very histrionic and we would just deal with it another day. So that was my first experience in court. It didn't go well. But as time passed, I became more comfortable doing things in court, and I got to watch really good lawyers do their best for their clients.

Much of the time, they were negotiating with the state attorneys. It was a little bit like horse trading or buying a used car. The state attorney would make a proposal, or the public defender would ask for a proposal from the state.

The two sides would go back and forth trying to reach an accommodation and get it done. You would then have to explain it to the client. We would frequently go out to the jail to meet with a client and explain to the client why it was in their best interest to enter a plea.

Once you entered the plea on a misdemeanor you had to be ready for them the client to be sentenced right then. In a felony, the judge would order what's called the pre-sentence investigation. You had to be ready to give your pitch to the judge as to why the client deserved some leniency. You would talk with the client to find out whatever their hard luck story might be. If they'd done good things in their life, you'd have to explain that to the court to try to get the best result for the client.

One of the things I learned was that most criminal clients are really not bad people. They are people who are in unfortunate circumstances and you almost have to try to help them both as a lawyer and as a social worker. You try to help them put their lives back together as best you can.

Being a public defender

When I graduated from law school, I tried to get a job with the Gainesville Public Defender's Office, where I had been clerking, but they hired a classmate of mine. I ended up applying and being hired by the Public Defender's Office in the Third Circuit, which was the group of counties immediately to the north. Their office was headquartered in Lake City.

Florida has 20 judicial circuits, most of which include multiple counties. In each circuit, under the constitution of the state of Florida, there's an elected public defender and an elected state attorney. The public defenders get a budget from the state of Florida and they hire assistant public defenders and staff as do the state attorneys.

The Third Circuit office in Lake City was different from the Gainesville office in that it was far more conservative. I stayed one year up there, and that job actually turned out to be a wonderful experience for me because I got to do all sorts of different areas of criminal law. The different divisions, for example in Gainesville, were traffic, misdemeanor, felony, and juvenile. And in the Third Circuit, on my first job, I got to do all of these and I got to do them all quickly.

Once they saw that I was minimally competent, they let me go without supervision to do my own caseload. So there I was—one year out of law school—and I was trying felony cases in front of juries and I was doing juvenile trials in front of judges, as well as misdemeanor and traffic cases.

Having grown up in the Northeast, I certainly didn't sound—and still don't sound—like your average resident of Suwannee County or Columbia County, which are very rural southern counties. But the state attorneys, the court personnel, and the sheriff's deputies were all very nice to me, even though they may have considered me sort of an alien being with my beard and non-southern accent.

And I must say, it was great working in a small town or series of small towns because you got to know the personnel and they got to know you. There's no substitute for having a sense of what a judge likes, or what a judge doesn't like, or even how to get admitted into a jail cell without waiting hours on end. You learn to be polite to all of the personnel. These may not be strictly legal lessons, but they're important lessons you have to learn as a lawyer: how to get along with people to get the best result possible.

Sometimes, as lawyers, we lose cases that we should win or expect to win and sometimes we win cases that we expect to lose. You never know exactly what a jury is going to do and how things are going to play out.

I learned that lesson a little bit when I won a case that I really had no business winning. It was during my time in the Third Circuit, up in Lake City, and since then I always since described it as the impossible case.

The impossible case

I was less than a year out of law school, and this was an armed robbery case. The defendants were two individuals who got off parole from Georgia. They were released from prison, came down to Florida, and decided to commit an armed robbery of a 7-Eleven in Lake City. It was classic criminal activity from criminals who weren't very bright.

They committed the robbery—I'm not sure where they got the firearm—at a 7-Eleven, then rushed out and got in their car. Unfortunately for them, the county's chief deputy was just driving right past when the call came into the Columbia County sheriff's office: "We've been robbed, we've been robbed."

The chief deputy was right there. He followed them to their mobile home where they had staged everything for the robbery. They parked, ran into the mobile home, threw off their clothes, and got changed. But there were five police cars out there. The sheriff's deputies took them into custody and brought them back to the jail. The deputies also took the clothing that had been discarded in the mobile home, and they did a lineup. You've seen plenty of lineups on TV. You put the suspects in a row with some other individuals and you have the victim of a crime see if they can pick out the perpetrator.

In this particular case, the officers were not sophisticated and they did exactly the wrong thing. They took the clothing that had been found in the trailer and they made the two suspects dress up in the jeans and denim jackets. The rest of the people in the lineup were dressed like bakers, wearing white pants and white t-shirts, the standard inmate uniform of the Columbia County Jail. Naturally, the victims picked out the two guys who were dressed as the robbers were dressed. Of course, these were the robbers anyway. Then, to memorialize this great bit of detective work, the crime-fighting deputies took photographs.

I was assigned to one of the defendants in this case and the other defendant hired a private attorney. The judge assigned to the case was new. He was very smart and very capable but he had not heard criminal cases before; this was his first criminal trial. I told him that I was filing what's called a motion to suppress. I argued, "Judge, this isn't fair. Here's a Supreme Court case on point. You can't have a lineup like this that's inherently unfair."

The state attorney who was prosecuting the case was a formidable fellow—he would later win fame for prosecuting Ted Bundy, among others—but in this case, he overreached. This is something that lawyers should never do, because when you overreach, you are setting yourself up for failure or an appellate reversal. Now of course, some lawyers try to gain an unfair advantage for their clients by overreaching, but it often doesn't work out. Doing the right thing, the honest thing, and the legal thing works better in the long run.

In this case the state attorney didn't agree with me. He argued to the judge that the lineup should not be suppressed. We went to trial and I was able to convince the jury in my closing argument that the identification was unfair, based on the photograph showing the two defendants dressed in the outfits of the robbers, with the rest of the lineup in white pants and white t-shirts.

Although the jury cut my client loose in this case, he was on parole from a prison sentence in Georgia, so he was held in jail. He was returned to Georgia and he was sent back to prison. Even though there was a not guilty jury determination in the robbery, there was still a separate parole violation and parole hearing, where the evidentiary standards would be a little different. He was convicted on the parole violation. Likewise, when his co-defendant was tried at a subsequent trial, he was convicted because the state attorney didn't make the same mistake a second time. He had seen the error of his ways and didn't overreach.

That was how I learned a lesson that you can win certain cases that you shouldn't. You do your best, you give it all you have, and generally the jury will do the right thing. In this case, it was the right thing to turn this individual loose, because the state and the deputies didn't do things the right way. You have to do it the right way. Of course, I've also seen instances where shortcuts or overreach worked, but I don't believe in them. I really don't—it's always better to do things right.

About three months after I took the job in Lake City, I was approached by Alan Parlapiano, the public defender back in Gainesville, about returning to Gainesville, where an opening had just come up. But I had given Milo Thomas, the public defender in Lake City, a one-year commitment, so I followed through on that.

After I completed my year in Lake City, my year in the Third Circuit, I accepted a job in the Eighth Circuit back in Gainesville.

Gainesville was the headquarters of the public defender's office for the Eighth Judicial Circuit, which included a number of different counties. I had gone to some of these out-counties, as we would call them. They're rural and more conservative than Alachua County, where Gainesville is located.

Alan Parlapiano hired me as the head of misdemeanor and traffic in the Gainesville Public Defender's Office. I also had an out-county; I had Levy County, which is a rural county sort of similar to the counties I had just come from in the Third Circuit.

After about a year in Gainesville, I was promoted to the felony division. Everyone in the public defender's office starts out in misdemeanor and traffic or juvenile. The goal is to get to the felony division because that's considered the big time. Those are the more serious crimes. A felony is a crime that can result in incarceration of more than one year in the state prison system.

At that point, I gave up my caseload of misdemeanor and traffic cases and picked up a caseload of felony cases. Our caseload would be about 80 felony cases. It's really hard work because every single month, you would have maybe 10 or 15 cases on what's called the trial docket. And you had to get all of those cases ready for trial.

Criminal cases are a little different from civil cases. In civil cases, you tell the judge when you're ready for trial. And typically, they're set out maybe eight to twelve months from when you tell the judge you're ready for trial. In criminal cases, the cases come up every month; they're driven by the judge setting them for trial at an arraignment. Although you can continue the cases, judges don't like to continue or postpone cases, so you have to be ready.

That means it's a fairly high burden having to be ready for trials. Either you have to meet with a client, negotiate a plea, change the plea, and then prepare for sentencing, or you have to be ready to try the cases. It was the same way in the Third Circuit, which is why I got some really good experience there trying cases because every month you were going to try a jury trial. That's really how you get experience as a lawyer, at least if you're going to be a litigator. It takes a lot of work to prepare for trial. You meet with the witnesses. You take their depositions. You file motions, which are requests of the court for certain things, for example, to exclude evidence, or exclude witnesses, or suppress evidence.

At any rate, as a felony attorney, I would have my 80 cases. They could include a mix of drug offenses, such as possession of marijuana, possession of cocaine, sale of marijuana, or sale of cocaine. They could be sex crimes. They could be sexual batteries. They could be worthless check cases. They could be armed robberies, or burglaries, or aggravated battery. They could be any one of a whole panoply of criminal activities, and we were working nonstop to try and represent, for the most part, poor individuals caught up in the criminal justice system.

Of course, a certain percentage of these cases aren't poor individuals caught up in the criminal justice system. There are career criminals or anti-social personalities, and those are often very difficult cases. Sometimes you're representing people that you do not admire, particularly in the sexual battery cases. But it's part of the job to do the best you could and get the best result for those individuals.

Suing the governor

The Eighth Circuit included Union and Bradford counties, which were noteworthy because they housed some of the state prisons. That included Florida State Prison, where death row prisoners were housed, and Union Correctional Institution. Those are prisons where you would get really difficult cases. The inmates would attack each other and they would attack the guards.

No one liked the inmates. The inmates frequently didn't like each other; the juries didn't like the inmates. It was really difficult working in those counties. I tried to avoid that particular assignment when I joined the Gainesville Public Defender's Office, but eventually I became involved in two significant cases that dealt specifically with the detention system.

While I was a felony attorney, I got involved with an issue came up from the juvenile attorneys. Their concern was that juveniles in the juvenile detention center were being assaulted by other more aggressive juvenile defendants. The reason for that was that there was no system of classification in the juvenile detention facility. Classification is very common now, but it wasn't common back then. Classification means assigning prisoners, or inmates, or juveniles into various locations, or pods, or living areas, according to the nature of the charges against them, their age, their physical ability, and other factors like that.

The idea is that you wouldn't put runaways or truants in a pod or living facility with armed robbers or rapists. But that's what the authorities at the juvenile detention center were doing, and as a result, the younger, more helpless children were being victimized, molested, and taken advantage of by older, more aggressive, more anti-social children, who may have had a variety of psychological disorders.

Juvenile attorneys, more than most defense attorneys, often seem joined at the hip with social workers and with psychologists. They're trying to help these kids out of really bad situations and provide for them so they don't turn into career criminals or feed into the criminal justice system. The juvenile attorneys in our office were very concerned about what was happening. They wanted the appropriate governmental agency to take action and establish some sort of classification system so the most helpless of these juveniles would not be constantly victimized.

All the requests to deal with the situation from an administrative point of view fell on deaf ears. We couldn't get the Department of Health and Rehabilitative Services (HRS) to do it voluntarily. So the decision was made to file a legal action on behalf of the kids, suing HRS and the state of Florida to force the issue.

Somehow I was drafted to participate in this, even though I wasn't a juvenile attorney, because they knew I could write legal briefs and memos, as well as argue different things. We had a hearing in front of a judge, who ended up being sympathetic to our cause. He understood what we were trying to do. He understood that what was happening was unreasonable, unnecessary, and horrible, so he granted our order forcing the state to implement a classification system for juveniles. The state, in its questionable wisdom, decided to appeal. So I was asked to do the appeal as well, and we were successful in the appeal.

After we succeeded in doing that appeal, a decision was made to undertake the same kind of legal action for the prisoners at Florida State Prison (FSP). The prisoners at FSP were a pretty bad bunch. You don't generally get sent to FSP for a first offense unless it's first degree murder. You have to work your way up. It's the worst of the worst—the worst-behaved prisoners with the worst sentences.

These individuals were attacking, assaulting, and even murdering each other frequently. The public defenders were overwhelmed, and they thought they needed to do something both to protect themselves and to protect the weaker inmates in the prison system. I was fairly inexperienced with the prison cases, so it was explained to me that the system didn't pay the guards, didn't train the guards well enough, and had never implemented a system-wide sweep for weapons. The inmates had a lot of homemade weapons.

So I was asked to sue the state on behalf of a bunch of murderers at FSP, and that's just what we did. At the very first hearing, in Starke, the county seat of Bradford County where the prison is located, we were told that the prisoners brought weapons to the courthouse. They wanted to show the judge how easy it was to smuggle weapons, not only into the prison but out of the prison. It turned out that the prisoners did indeed have a lot of homemade shanks with them. We were shocked. We took the weapons and showed them to the judge, and the judge was shocked.

The judge was Judge R.A. Green, Jr., known as Buzzy Green. He appointed a special master to investigate the Florida Prison System. His appointee was a professor at the University of Florida who had formerly run the entire US Department of Prisons. The role of the special master was to investigate the prison system, specifically at FSP, and determine what could be done better.

Well, once Judge Green made this ruling, he essentially took control of the prison. He indicated that no new prisoners could be added to the prison. He imposed a population cap, and the Florida Department of Corrections (DOC) was very upset that a member of the judiciary had essentially taken control of this executive responsibility.

So DOC appealed, and Mr. Parlapiano, my boss, who was the elected public defender for the Eighth Circuit, was called up to Tallahassee by the Attorney General of the state of Florida. I was only two years or three years out of law school. I'd never even been to Tallahassee, which is our state capital. As I was the lead attorney on this case both in the trial court and in the appeal, Alan brought me with him up to Tallahassee. We were ushered into this giant corner office in the capitol building, and in the office was Jim Smith, the Attorney General of the state of Florida.

He made us feel comfortable, and then he laid down the law: "You know, you're state employees. You're employed by the state of Florida. Your boss is the Governor. You can't sue the Governor. You can't sue the state of Florida. You need to drop this lawsuit immediately." I'm paraphrasing, but that was the gist of it.

Fortunately for me, my boss, Mr. Parlapiano, had balls of steel, or to put it more politely, he was a profile in courage. Alan looked at Jim Smith and said, very politely, "I have a responsibility as public defender, and we'll make our own decisions, but we'll certainly consider what you've said." And we left.

The end result was we pursued our lawsuit. The name of the case was Graham v. Vann. Bob Graham was the Governor of Florida. We sued Bob Graham and Louie Wainwright, who was the head of the Florida Department of Corrections.

When there is an appeal, the appellate court has the right to have the attorneys make an oral argument in front of them. In this case, the First District Court of Appeals wanted to hear from the attorneys. Fortunately for me, I got to do the oral argument. It was quite an experience, to be arguing an appeal, particularly since I was only two years out of law school and this was the first appeal I'd ever seen.

Arguing an appeal turned out to be a little bit like being in law school. You start with a brief presentation; you're up there at a podium for 20 minutes and there's a clock counting down your time. Then the judges—three of them in this case—start peppering you with questions about why should they rule with you, and what the particular issues in your case are about.

But when we got to the First District Court of Appeal that day, we were told—me and the Assistant Attorney General, who was arguing the case for the state—that because this was such an important case, the judges had rearranged their schedule. There were no other cases for the day and we could take as long as we wanted.

So we argued our case in front of the First District and we won the case. They ruled for us against Governor Graham and Secretary Wainwright, and the judge implemented the reforms recommended by the special master that he had appointed. You could find the case at 394 So.2d 176 (Fla. 1DCA 1981).

This case was a bit of a turning point for me. Working on this case gave me a taste for civil procedure and civil cases. It wasn't exactly a typical civil case, but it certainly wasn't a criminal case, and when I eventually decided to go into private practice I moved away from criminal cases to the civil cases I still do now.

Private practice

After about four years, I left the public defender's office. I wasn't really sure what I wanted to do. I moved into an office and basically took whatever came in the door. This was in the early '80s. I was sharing space with some other lawyers, and they were very helpful to me. It was really great, in a small town like Gainesville, how the lawyers were willing to share their knowledge and help young lawyers in many ways.

I am particularly grateful to Vic Hulslander and Dan O'Connell, two former assistant public defenders. I didn't know much about the civil cases that I was starting to explore, so I would wander down to their office and ask them questions, and they really helped me.

Eventually, my former colleague, Tom Farkash, who had been an assistant public defender with me, came and joined me. We started doing criminal cases, and family law cases, and basically any kind of case that would come through the door.

After the first few years in private practice, I also invited my former boss Alan Parlapiano to join our law firm. The reason I had invited my first partner, Tom Farkash, and then Alan to join us, is that they were two of the best lawyers that I knew. The public defender's office, when I was there, was full of really good trial lawyers. Their skills were considerably better than mine. Every lawyer has their own skill set—that skill set may be a great ability to cross-examine, or a great ability to write, or a great ability just to talk to people and be intuitive. What's really important is to make the best of your own skill set so you can be successful. There are many ways to be successful as an attorney.

With Tom and Alan, I knew from working with them in the public defender's office that they really had skill in the courtroom, they were very bright, and we were all basically aligned in terms of how you approach a case—what needs to be done and how you do it. We all wanted to help each individual client as much as we could. We believed that economic success would follow just by doing a really good job for clients and working really hard. Maybe that's not always the case, but we thought it was and it seemed to work out that way for us. Gradually, we moved away from criminal defense, which was where we had been most comfortable. We began doing more and more personal injury cases, including brain injury cases and premises liability cases, until we got to the point where we were doing exclusively personal injury cases. And we've continued doing those to this day.

We also restored and moved into an old historic office building on which we spent a lot of time. Tom Farkash and I learned that there was an old Victorian house for sale a few blocks away from our office. We realized it would be an ideal law office, so we decided to buy the house, renovate it, and make it our office. Tom and I bought the building, and we just spent hours and hours on the plans to restore it. We actually did a little bit of the physical work ourselves until we saw that—for me at least—an aching body from stripping wood was not worth it and I should incline my pursuits to funding the workers who were better at it than I was.

The building was pretty dilapidated when we bought it in 1982, and the renovations took almost two years. We are still very proud of the fact that our purchase and preservation of the house actually helped to preserve other historic buildings in the neighborhood. When we were considering buying the building, there were architects who owned the historic buildings on either side of it. They wanted to buy the whole block, tear down the old buildings, and build a big, modern office building. But our purchase and restoration of that house put an end to those plans.

Our firm still works in that house today, and our office has been part of Historic Gainesville tours.

My two partners have retired and now my wife Cherie and my daughter Julie are practicing with me. Our firm has become a real family affair, and that's a joy for me. It's a privilege to work with them as we seek justice for our clients.

Chapter 2: Why You Need an Attorney When You Are Injured

I'VE SPENT my entire adult life around lawyers and the law. So to me, contacting a lawyer after an accident or injury is the most natural thing in the world. But I understand that the average person doesn't have much experience with lawyers. Maybe you've had a lawyer help you draft a will, or maybe you've been through a divorce, but if not, you may have never even met a lawyer. So you may not even think of contacting an attorney after an accident.

Let me share a couple of stories that may change your thinking about that: These stories illustrate how representatives of the "system" are prejudiced and biased against the injured victim.

I was a young lawyer starting out doing personal injury cases, and an elderly African-American man—we'll call him Mr. Smith—came to see me. He said, "Mr. Fine, I think I need your help. I don't know what to do. I can't see a doctor. I was in an accident, and I can't see a doctor."

I asked him what he meant and he said, "Well, the insurance company is telling me I can't see a doctor." This made absolutely no sense to me. Florida is what we call a "no fault" state, which means that no matter who's at fault in a car accident, your own insurance company pays for you to see a doctor. At that time, there was a $10,000 limit, and the company would pay 80 percent of medical bills. So what Mr. Smith was telling me about the insurance company seemed very unlikely, but I probed a little further.

I took Mr. Smith's case, opened a file, and began to investigate. I got the accident report, which showed that it was a car accident and that Mr. Smith clearly was not at fault. So why was his medical care being disallowed?

Florida law allows an insurance company to do what's called a <u>compulsory medical evaluation (CME)</u>. It used to be called an independent medical evaluation (IME). If after months of treatment the insurance company thinks that the rehabilitation process is being abused, or an individual is seeing a chiropractor too many times, or thinks there's some other irregularity, the company could send an individual to the company's own doctor.

I called the local adjuster for Mr. Smith's insurance company, and he told me they had sent Mr. Smith for an IME. And I said, "What do you mean you sent him for an IME? He had been in the accident five days earlier. You can't send him for a cutoff under a theory that he's abusing the medical care five days after the accident. That's totally inappropriate! You just can't do that!"

Well, the adjuster backed down, but what had happened in this case is the adjuster took advantage of this elderly African-American man, thinking he could cut off his benefits, and this injured accident victim wouldn't know any better. It was just a really blatant and, in my opinion, racist and unfortunate action by the insurance company.

With one phone call and some justified indignation on my part, I was able to reverse that decision because I threatened the adjuster and told him I would file a lawsuit. There was no question that we would win; what he was doing was abusing the process. There was no question in my mind that it was a total abuse of the system.

That's just one example of why an individual needs a lawyer: Insurance companies will take advantage of you anytime they see an opening. In Mr. Smith's case, the adjuster thought he saw an obvious opening. This client was unsophisticated, and the insurance company was trying to take advantage of him.

I wish I could say that things have gotten better, but they have not. Let's fast-forward about 25 years. I'm representing a client who was rear-ended in two separate collisions, and he saw the doctor. The client—we'll call him Mr. Davis—had some obvious evidence of injury. Some months down the road, Mr. Davis ended up having surgery for nerve damage in his arm.

I had made a recovery against the wrongdoer's insurance company for $25,000, which was their limit, and then I made what's called an uninsured motorist (UM) claim against Mr. Davis's insurance company.

When you take out UM coverage in your policy, whether it's underinsured motorist or uninsured motorist, that coverage is intended to protect you if you're injured and the wrongdoer's insurance policy doesn't have enough coverage.

Mr. Davis's insurance carrier was a large, nationally-known company. And the company's position was that Mr. Davis, who was a small business owner in his fifties, wasn't really hurt. They thought the case was weak, so they offered only $2,500 on each incident because there were two separate accidents within about six months.

We filed the lawsuit. The case was set for trial, and because I was very busy with another case that was going to trial the next month, my wife and daughter volunteered to represent Mr. Davis.

Very often an insurance company will offer more money if you litigate a case. The company doubled its offer $5,000 for each incident, then increased the offer again to $10,000 for each incident, a total of $20,000 in a proposal for settlement (PFS). The PFS is a pleading which can be done by either side. If the defense gets 25 percent less in court than they propose, the plaintiff pays their attorney fees. If we get 25 percent more than we propose, the defense pays our attorney fees.

Mr. Davis was determined to have his day in court because he thought he was really hurt, and his own insurance company was standing against him. They hired two different doctors to testify that Mr. Davis wasn't really hurt, essentially claiming that he was making it up and that all his injuries were degenerative in nature. Well, Cherie and Julie tried the case, and the jury came back with a verdict of $438,000.

Now, on top of that $438,000, we're going receive for Mr. Davis another couple hundred thousand dollars in attorney fees because we filed a PFS that we beat by more than 25 percent. In fact, we beat it by approximately 400 percent.

Why am I telling these stories in a chapter about why an individual needs an attorney? The most important reason why an individual, an accident victim, needs an attorney to represent him or her is that the insurance companies will try to take advantage of the accident victim. The system is slanted against the plaintiff and in favor of the insurance companies.

How the system favors insurance companies in large and small ways

Nonjoinder statute—One of the reasons why we were so successful in Mr. Davis's case was that it was a UM case, and so we were able to name the insurance company. Normally, you can't name the insurance company in a case. When you file suit, you file it against the wrongdoer, not against the insurance company. Florida law has a nonjoinder statute, which means that if I hurt someone in an accident, and I have a great insurance policy, the jury won't hear about it. The theory is that if a jury knows that there's an insurance policy, they're more likely to return a larger verdict.

Insurance company resources—The insurance companies have much greater resources than any average individual has. They can afford to decide that they're going to underpay on a given case, and it doesn't really affect them if Jack Fine or Cherie Fine or Julie Fine gets a $400,000 verdict on a case that might be worth $20,000. They have millions and millions of dollars. But it certainly affects the client if the case is going to drag out for a year or two or three years. He needs that few thousand dollars that he can get in the settlement, and he can't afford to take the gamble of a PFS that comes back against him, leaving him owing the insurance company thousands of dollars.

The insurance companies' sheer size and tremendous financial resources work in their favor, but it's more than that. In my opinion, these companies made a decision 20 or 30 years ago that, from a business point of view, they would make more money underpaying claims than paying them fairly. Of course, the law says they're supposed to use good faith in evaluating claims, and under certain circumstances they can be subject to extra damages for failure to negotiate claims in good faith. But that's extremely difficult to prove. So as a result of the insurance companies being corporations interested in their bottom line, they have determined, as a regular course of business practice, to be unfair to the individual claimant. That's how they run their business. That's how they make money.

The companies also use that money to hire their own experts and doctors. Once an orthopedist or a neurologist is on an insurance company payroll, there's no doctor–patient relationship that applies, and it is natural human nature to reward the individual who pays you. It's no longer a question of their Hippocratic Oath but loyalty to their employer.

A radiologist who interprets x-rays and MRIs and CT scans, for example, is usually just sitting in an office somewhere. They don't know whether the patient is a plaintiff in a personal injury case or an individual who has seen a private doctor. They can just call it as they see it; it's what's called a blind read, an objective opinion. But the radiologists who work for the insurance companies generally take the position that would benefit the insurance companies. They know it's an insurance case; they know who sent them the scan; and they know who is paying their bill. What happens is that they are more likely to report that the injury is degenerative, not traumatic, or that they just don't see an injury. Then it's up to the plaintiff's lawyer to depose and defeat that doctor in a trial setting.

Advertising and Lobbying—Insurance companies pay millions of dollars every year, both in their advertising and their government lobbying, to make the system better work for them. It's an organized and well-funded propaganda campaign that has been going on for decades.

What does all this mean to someone who's been in an accident? It means is you can't rely on an insurance company to treat you fairly, and because you can't rely on an insurance company to treat you fairly, you need someone on your side.

Now, it's easy enough for someone to accuse me of exaggerating because I'm a plaintiff's lawyer. I represent individuals, so I speak from my own particular perspective. But I also have the benefit of almost 40 years of practicing law, and this is my deeply held conviction. It's based on my own experience, seeing what actually happens day in and day out as I negotiate cases on behalf of individuals whose lives have been turned topsy-turvy as a result of their injuries. We try to do the right thing on behalf of these individuals, and the insurance companies are our adversaries. And they almost always do their very best to underpay valid claims.

It is an adversary system

People in their day-to-day life try to get along. It is part of our culture to work together and treat others in a fair manner. The insurance claims system and our legal system have an adversarial basis that can be difficult to understand. The desire of an accident victim to be treated fairly is fundamentally different than the goal of the insurance company. An attorney can help the innocent victim be compensated through knowledgeable advocacy.

Corporate structure and purpose

An insurance company is a corporation. Its purpose is to make money and grow the company. One means of doing that is to limit the amount of claims. Many times the insurance companies rate their adjusters by their average claim payment. There are internal corporate incentives to pay out less in claims. Who gets hurt by this policy? The injured plaintiff.

Attorneys can alleviate stress

There are a lot of moving pieces in a personal injury case, and that can be overwhelming for anyone, especially someone dealing with the aftermath of an accident or injury. When I first shifted from doing criminal law to personal injury cases, even the vocabulary itself seemed somewhat foreign to me. I didn't know the difference between PIP and UM. I didn't know what collision coverage was. There were a lot of technical terms and different considerations that even I, as an experienced lawyer, had to learn about.

The average client who has been in an accident is dealing with unfamiliar concepts and unfamiliar situations. They have to deal with property damage. They have to deal with a rental car. They have to deal with pain, with inability to work, with lost income. They may have family members who are in these situations as well. They need help. They're under stress.

A lawyer can help relieve that stress. It's hard enough to recover from an injury when your body has been subjected to trauma. The more stress an individual has when they've been hurt, the worse it is.

The worse the injury, the more help an individual needs. We must be, as lawyers, sympathetic to what an individual is going through. Maybe there's a traumatic brain injury. The individual is hospitalized in a coma and the family members are assembled in the hospital. They don't know what to do. They don't know where to turn. They have questions about life support. They have questions about who's going to pay the bills. They have questions about who's going to care for the children while their loved one is hospitalized or comatose.

The lawyer can help with all these issues. Can he solve all the problems? No. But an experienced lawyer who has been through these situations before can give valuable guidance. If an individual receives a spinal cord injury that leaves them quadriplegic or paraplegic, they don't know what's in store for them. They don't know about rehabilitation hospitals. They don't know about the spinal cord injury fund that's been set up by the State of Florida. They don't know how it all works. The attorney can give them guidance as they work their way through the system from a medical point of view, a psychological and emotional point of view, and a legal point of view.

The role of the attorney is essentially the same even if the injury is not as severe. In every case, we're giving guidance. We're trying to relieve stress. We're trying to help the individual cope with a system that is foreign to them. By giving a family member or an injured victim a sense of what lies ahead, the attorney helps to alleviate psychological and systemic stress and support the individual in an extremely difficult situation. That's what we try to do, and that's why I believe you need an attorney when you have been injured.

Points to Remember

1. As an accident victim you are in an adversarial system.

2. The system is slanted against you.

3. An attorney can help you navigate through the pitfalls.

4. An attorney can help alleviate stress.

Chapter 3: How to Hire an Attorney

MOST PEOPLE who come to our office don't have what I would call a family attorney. They've been in an accident, they have a problem, and very often a friend or a relative, or sometimes another attorney, will refer them. They don't know us. An individual who's in an accident is really on his own to figure out how to find and hire an attorney.

The first question is, do you need an attorney? As a general rule, if you're going to be dealing with an insurance company, it's going to be an adversarial situation, and at least talking to an attorney is a good idea. The attorney can help you determine whether you need representation.

How do you find an attorney?

The best way to hire an attorney is talk to several people who've been injured and have gone through the legal process. Most people don't shop around and go from one attorney to another, sizing them up. They're usually going to hire the attorney in the first office they go to. If you are not going to meet with multiple prospective attorneys it is important to do some research and ask some questions before making a choice.

The individual is often at a disadvantage because they haven't been through this before. Anyone in the attorney's office is going to seem knowledgeable because they speak the vocabulary that's common in these kinds of cases, and they will have some degree of knowledge.

But finding the best attorney is difficult because a lot of attorneys advertise, but not a lot of attorneys try cases. You'll find plenty of law firm advertising anywhere you look. But just picking someone out of a hat based on advertising is probably the worst way to hire an attorney.

Why? Because you don't know what you're going to get. Some of the large law firms that have offices in multiple cities have some really good attorneys, but very often those really good attorneys won't work on the cases that come into the office seeking immediate attention. Many larger firms will designate a paralegal, or legal secretary, or some kind of case manager to deal with the case in its pre-litigation stages.

An individual accident victim needs to know who's going to be dealing with the case. Will it going to be a licensed attorney, or is it going to be someone with a high school education or less, and really no certification whatsoever?

There are differences among licensed attorneys. Consult rating services such as Martindale/Hubble and Avvo. Attorneys who are members of invitation-only trial lawyers' groups such as the American Board of Trial Advocates (ABOTA) are qualified by a wealth of experience. Look into the organizations listed on an attorney's resumé. Of course, even a highly qualified attorney cannot help you if preliminary issues are delegated to an overworked staff.

Just last week, a young man came in to see me, painfully holding his hand. He told me he had a fracture as a result of an auto accident. And aside from the emergency room, he hadn't been seen by a doctor in 30 days. He had an attorney; he was coming to me for a second opinion. I told him that he was better off sticking with his own attorney because there could be some additional costs associated with discharging his first attorney. Everyone has a right to do that, of course. All it takes is a one-sentence letter telling the attorney they are discharged, but then you're liable for the time that they've spent on the case so far, unless it is within three days of hiring an attorney or there is just cause for his discharge. Of course, in his case, probably no attorney had spent any time on the case.

The problem was no one had paid attention. This was a large firm, which advertised a lot, but he had never even talked to an attorney. In fact, there wasn't an attorney assigned as far as I know. A paralegal was assigned to his case, and he had talked with her a couple times, but she didn't return his calls. They couldn't get him to an orthopedic surgeon to look at the finger fracture. This injured accident victim was a maintenance worker, and he couldn't work, so he had no income coming in. He really needed help. I met with him, along with my assistant, and we came up with a plan of action. We were able to get this client scheduled to see an orthopedist to take a look at the fractures in his hand, and continue to see the neurologist that he'd originally been referred to. He ended up discharging the first lawyer and hiring us.

The point I want to make is that he went to a "lawyer." He went to a firm that specializes in accident cases, but the office setup didn't have a lawyer looking at the case. I could be a great lawyer. I could be highly skilled in trial, but if I don't spend the time talking to a client about their problems and customizing an immediate solution for the aftermath of the crash, then I'm not doing my job. In this case, that law office didn't do their job and they lost that particular client.

There was a judge I appeared in front of when I was a young lawyer in the public defender's office. His name was Judge John J Crews. I thought Judge Crews was great because he was knowledgeable and he was fair. On his wall, Judge Crews had an old English print that said, "A lawyer's time and advice is his stock in trade." I think that rings true today. The lawyer has to spend time and give good advice to a client. In looking for a lawyer, look for someone who has some degree of experience, but just as important, someone who is willing to spend the time and effort to analyze the client's situation, and provide the best advice.

The most important thing you can do is make the initial call. If you think you might need an attorney, pick up the phone and call an attorney. The advantage of the personal injury attorney is that unlike a family law attorney, or a criminal attorney, or a real estate attorney, we don't bill by the hour. As a matter of fact, we don't bill at all unless we sign a contingent fee contract. This is one of the few areas where you can get free advice. It doesn't cost you anything other than a few minutes of your time to call an attorney.

It's important to take positive steps to hire the right attorney. Don't be afraid to ask as many questions as come to mind. Look at the attorney's website. Look at other attorneys' websites. You may not make heads or tails of their qualifications from the websites, but actually getting them on the phone and talking with them is generally a good idea. If the attorney isn't willing to talk with you, or the person who gets on the phone sounds like they don't know what they're doing, that's a red flag and you should stay away from that office.

What should you ask before you hire an attorney?

Unfortunately, it's difficult for the public to size up who's a good attorney and who's a bad attorney. Here are some questions to consider.

<u>What kind of law do they practice?</u> Look for someone who specializes in personal injury law. A generalist—someone who does some family law, maybe a little bit of criminal law—won't know the key issues as well as a specialist who deals with personal injury cases every day. I think you're better typically with a specialist in an area like personal injury, someone who's familiar with the issues of soft tissue injuries, spinal injuries, brain injuries and fractures. Make sure they have litigated cases involving the identical issues and injuries involved in your case. Those lawyers know what these cases are about. They know who the good doctors are. They know who the bad doctors are. They know what the key issues are and they know how to get the best for you.

<u>How well do they know your community?</u> In Florida, for instance, an attorney might be based in another city. Maybe they're based in Orlando and they advertise in Ocala. Well, the attorney who has grown up in Ocala, who has practiced there for 15 years or 20 years, knows the location of the city streets and the traffic patterns. They know the doctors. They know the judges. They know the local defense lawyers. All other things being equal, it is my belief that a local attorney is going to do better for you than someone in another city who's not familiar with your locale, the physicians, or the

court personnel. So you want to know where the attorney is from and where they are practicing.

How will they handle your case? You should ask about the experience of the lawyer, but even more importantly, you should ask whether the lawyer will actually handle the case. In many larger firms, lawyers don't handle the case; a case manager does. A lawyer may not get involved unless and until litigation begins.

In our firm, the lawyer makes all the decisions in the pre-litigation cases, as well as in the trial cases. Of course, the client makes the final decision as to whether to settle the case or not. But as a consumer of legal services, an accident victim or someone acting on the accident victim's behalf, you need to know how things are going to be paid for, the experience of the lawyer, and whether the lawyer's actually going to handle the case.

We have lawyers at every step of the process. One of the reasons for that is that we believe it's important for the lawyer to get to know the client, and we believe that process begins at the beginning of the case.

Every case is different. And every case has its unique challenges, such as finding an orthopedic surgeon for an individual who doesn't have insurance when the original hospitalization used up all the coverage. What do you do? How do you proceed? Well, a lawyer, due to his or her experience, is going to have a better sense of what to do and how to proceed than someone who has only a high school education. That's not to disparage assistants who are extremely well trained, but it's not the same thing. And the public doesn't always understand that.

<u>Do they litigate cases?</u> A lawyer may tell you that they've handled many cases like yours, and that's good, but it's not enough. You need to ask whether they litigate cases. That's important for two reasons. Number one, a lawyer who doesn't litigate cases will not be able to get the same result from an insurance company. These insurance companies pay more when they realize there's a lawyer who can and will hold their feet to the fire. Number two, a lawyer who doesn't litigate cases may try to get the client to settle because they know they will lose the fee, or at least a portion of the fee, if the case is litigated and they can't settle it.

Many lawyers simply don't want to litigate. When I say <u>litigate</u>, I mean file a lawsuit and go forward with the case. There are plenty of reasons for that. Litigation is hard. It's stressful; it costs a lot of money and it costs a lot of time. It's much easier to sit back, make a few phone calls, and settle a case than it is to actually go to court, see the judge at a pre-trial hearing, do the discovery, take depositions, and file motions to compel because the insurance companies are hiding critical pieces of evidence and you have to dig it out of them with a court order. That's not easy, and a lot of lawyers don't want to do it.

So in addition to making sure that the lawyer has experience, and that an actual lawyer will be handling the case, it's important to find someone who will actually file the lawsuit if the case calls for it. You also want a lawyer who has sufficient financial resources to invest in the appropriate experts and sufficient experience to know the right experts, along with the ability and initiative to go out and find the right expert if they don't know the right expert. All of that takes effort, money, and time. You want a lawyer who will put all of those things into your case.

Most importantly, you want a lawyer that you can talk to—someone you will feel comfortable with sharing all the personal details of your case—someone who will sit down and take the time to talk with you. I believe there's no better way to learn about the case than talking to the client personally.

I like it when a client comes in to see me multiple times. Other lawyers might not like that; they may be bothered and not want to meet with the client. I find that the more times I meet with a client, the better job I can do for that client. You have to get to know the client in order to advocate effectively for them.

Once you have decided upon a lawyer, the next step is to put a contract in place with that lawyer.

The personal injury contract

The state of Florida has a personal injury contract which is largely standardized, and it is very beneficial to the injured party. The personal injury contract is a contingent fee contract (see Exhibit A), which means that an individual does not have to expend any money out of pocket to hire the lawyer. When you go to a law office, you can seek out the lawyer with the best reputation in town, and hire a really good lawyer with no immediate cost to you. The contract does provide that there will be a fee if the lawyer makes a recovery on behalf of the client. The recovery is the contingency. The contingent fee is typically one-third of the recovery; it goes up to 40 percent if there's extensive litigation and 45 percent if there's an appeal.

The lawyers certainly are paid for their work. Sometimes they are overpaid, and sometimes they are underpaid. When we open a file, we don't know how much work the case is going to take. If a lawyer puts in hundreds of hours on a case, it goes to trial, and he loses the case, he could lose not only the hundreds of hours of time, but also tens of thousands of dollars in costs. The lawyer typically advances costs on behalf of a client—for things like medical records, depositions, expert witnesses, interviews with physicians, travel if we have to go out of state. All these costs are advanced by the lawyer.

The standard contract does provide that the costs are subtracted from the client's share after the lawyer takes his fee. For example, if there's a $10,000 recovery, and the case isn't litigated, the lawyer will take a one-third fee, which is $3,333, and the client will get the balance minus whatever the lawyer has spent on the case. If it's a non-litigation case, the costs will usually be just a few hundred dollars for medical records or miscellaneous expenses. In a major case though, the costs could be significant. And also, remember that the no fault law in the state of Florida provides for something called personal injury protection (PIP), which pays 80 percent of the first $10,000 in medical expenses. What that means is that there's a 20 percent balance up to $10,000, and that too must be paid out of the funds that we obtain for a client.

That's why it's really important for the lawyer to inform the client what the bottom line is before settling a case. Along with the attorney's fee contract that sets forth the percentages, there's a separate document called a statement of client's rights that we are required to furnish to the clients (see Exhibit B). The lawyer signs it and the client signs it and is provided a copy.

The first right is that there's no legal requirement that a lawyer charge a client a set fee. You have the right to talk to the lawyer about the fee and negotiate. If you don't reach an agreement with one lawyer, you may talk with other lawyers. Most lawyers are not going to want to reduce their fee. Sometimes we'll do that, but most of the time, lawyers know that a case can end up being an extraordinary amount of work and they're going to want to use the standard fee. Any contingency fee contract must be in writing, and you have three business days to reconsider the contract. You can cancel a contract without any reason if you notify your lawyer in writing within three business days of signing a statement.

Before signing a contingency fee contract with you, the lawyer must advise you whether he intends to handle the case alone or whether other lawyers will be helping with the case. If the lawyer intends to refer the case, he needs to advise you of that. Some firms that don't try cases will refer all their trial cases out to an attorney, so you'll be getting a new attorney if the case needs to be tried. But once again, there's going to be pressure. They don't want to refer the case to a new attorney because they're going to lose a significant portion of their fees, so they're going to put pressure on the client to settle, and that's not good.

You have the right to be told about possible adverse consequences if you lose the case. If you think the lawyer is charging you an excessive fee, the Florida bar can be called in. You also have the right to make a final decision regarding a case.

- You have the right to know about the experience of your lawyer.

- You have the right to be advised how the costs are going to be paid.
- You have the right to know what's happening in your case at any time.
- You have the right to terminate this contract within the first three days at no cost to you.

Points to Remember

1. Talk to an attorney not a "case manager."

2. Ratings and experience do matter.

3. Hire a specialist.

4. Hire a litigator.

Chapter 4: How a Personal Injury Case Proceeds

IN THE NORMAL COURSE of a case, an individual comes to see me after an accident or injury of some kind—it may be an auto accident, or a trip and fall, or some other injury, or some other premises liability situation.

When a client first comes in to our office, they've probably never been in this situation before. The client doesn't know about the various provisions in the insurance policy. He doesn't what to do about a rental car. He doesn't know where he should go for medical care. There are just so many decisions to make.

In some cases the individual has received medical treatment and in some they haven't.

If the injury is really serious and they've already had surgery or they're being treated by a specialist, I make a strong effort not to interfere with their medical care. Most of the time the specialists in town—the surgeons, orthopedists, and neurosurgeons—are highly qualified; they doing a good job and they already know the patient. I don't want to interfere with that.

On the other hand, if it's an injury where they've been treated and released by the hospital, whether or not they've been instructed to seek follow-up care, I will frequently offer the client some alternative suggestions for treatment. That's because the treatment decisions are really important.

The decision about which doctor to see is important because under state law in automobile accident cases a doctor needs to say there's a permanent injury in order for the individual victim to be able to make a recovery for his pain and suffering, in other words, for non-economic damages.

A lot of doctors are simply unwilling to treat individuals who've been in car accident cases or are involved in litigation. It's not because the doctors are uncaring or don't like the patient. It's simply the fact that litigation is a time-consuming, sometimes energy-sapping business for the individual physician who gets involved. The doctors want to treat patients; they don't want to be involved with lawyers.

There can be scheduling problems, there can be payment problems, and there can be all sorts of reasons why they don't want to be involved with lawyers. What we try to do is give the client choices among doctors we know who are competent and who are willing to treat in these kinds of cases. Most of the doctors who treat initially will end up referring out to specialists and they have specialists lined up who are willing to treat in these cases.

Another consideration is helping clients do not have insurance, or whose PIP has run out, and are unable to pay for needed medical care. Sometimes we can help them find a doctor who will treat them and not charge them until the end of their case. That's called treating on a <u>letter of protection</u>, which basically says that the doctor will be paid out of any recovery if we make a recovery. Now, the doctor is taking a chance there; it's the equivalent of the lawyer's contingency agreement. But if the doctor knows and respects the lawyer, and knows that a recovery is likely in this lawyer's cases, they're willing to take that chance.

A typical case

Here's what typically happens when a client comes to see me. We'll have a session where I get to know the client and their background, and then I explain how these cases work and the general timeline. We go over the personal injury contract and the statement of clients' rights, as I described in the previous chapter. The state of Florida requires us to do that. If the client signs a retainer agreement, we will open a file and begin working up the case.

If needed, we will offer the client suggestions for treatment, as mentioned above. In the meantime, while the treatment is going on, we're contacting the insurance company and we're doing an investigation on how the accident happened, to determine liability. We may be contacting witnesses; we may be hiring experts. We take some of the stress of the preliminary work-up of the case off the client. The client just needs to see the right doctor, get the right treatment, and focus on dealing with his or her injuries.

We contact the insurance company to ascertain what the coverage is. We send them an initial <u>letter of representation</u> and request for the policy. In Florida the insurance company is required to disclose the insurance policy to the attorney for the claimant or the accident victim. So within 30 days, in most cases, they will send us the policy. In some cases we have to be more aggressive because the insurance companies are not always compliant with the law. But one way or another we will get the policy. Sometimes there are multiple policies that apply to any one accident. The attorney should obtain all the policies.

At that point there are essentially two different ways to proceed with a personal injury case. Most commonly, the individual client undergoes his treatment and reaches an endpoint in his treatment which is <u>Maximum Medical Improvement</u>, or MMI. Once a client reaches MMI the doctor sends us what's called an <u>impairment rating</u>.

The impairment rating is written according to guidelines published by the American Medical Association. After the doctor gives us an impairment rating for the patient, we send a <u>demand letter</u> to the insurance company. The letter is actually more of a package. It includes copies of all the records—everything that has to do with the case—including the accident report, photographs, sometimes tax records, employment records, and all the medical billings. That's where we put forward a demand, a time-limited demand, to the insurance company. If the insurance company makes an offer, we then communicate that offer to the client. It often happens that we reject their first offer—and frequently their second offers and third offers—and negotiate back and forth with the insurance company to reach a settlement.

That's one way these cases get resolved. It can take anywhere from three or four months up to a maximum of twelve to eighteen months. The time varies because it's hard to negotiate and get the best result until the client is at maximum medical improvement. We need to see what the medical bills are, what the injuries are, what the future impact is, and what has been taken from the client.

Going to litigation

The second way to proceed in these cases is to file a lawsuit immediately, or almost immediately. Why would we want to file a lawsuit quickly in a case? Experience has taught us that being more aggressive with the insurance companies pays dividends for the client. I can cite many cases where the pre-litigation offers were minimal, but the act of bringing suit, even if it didn't go to trial, produced a better result for the client.

An example is a case I recently settled at a <u>mediation</u>, which is a settlement conference. The client was a young woman who was injured in two relatively low-speed accidents. Before we filed the lawsuit the offer was under $10,000 and the case settled at a mediation for $50,000. So by filing the lawsuit we increased the offer by a factor of five.

If we take the first track—sending a demand package to the insurance company—and the company comes back with an inadequate offer, we can always litigate the case at that point. But by then a year has passed and once we've filed suit it's frequently another year before the case either goes to trial or gets mediated. That's why we sometimes just go ahead and file the lawsuit, knowing that they take us more seriously when a lawsuit is filed.

What's the downside of filing a lawsuit? Of course you could lose if you go to court. But usually if the lawsuit is filed, you will be given an opportunity to settle the case for an amount in excess of what was offered before the suit was filed.

Some cases are obviously litigation cases, especially where the injury is significant. We would then advise the client to file right away, because that's the way to maximize the value of the case. When we file a suit, the contingent fee goes up from one third to 40 percent. We start incurring costs in the case, beginning with a filing fee that is usually about $500, so we better be able to increase the offer and we almost always significantly increase the offer when we file the lawsuit.

Litigation does require the attorney to work harder. There's just no comparison between cases with and without litigation. The litigation cases take far more work. And this goes back to the issue of hiring a lawyer. It's really important that you hire a lawyer or a law firm that is willing to litigate cases. There's a huge difference between hiring a lawyer who always tries to settle cases and a lawyer who is willing to litigate cases. The difference can be literally tens of thousands of dollars or even hundreds of thousands of dollars in the client's pocket.

You want a lawyer who is not only willing to litigate, but who also has experience litigating. There's no substitute for experience in litigation. A lawyer has to know the personalities of the judges, the rules of procedure, and the rules of evidence and apply this knowledge to the specific issues, both medical and legal, in the case. You only gain this knowledge through experience, study, and collaborative effort.

Different defense lawyers also have different approaches to a case. An experienced lawyer will recognize defense lawyers who are being very difficult and will tailor their approach accordingly.

Another thing we mentioned in terms of hiring a lawyer is that you need someone who can and will spend money on experts when it is warranted. That's important when your case is being litigated.

For example, we recently handled a case where the client had a mild traumatic brain injury. We hired a neurologist, who recommended a test called Diffusion Tensor Imaging, or DTI. It's a diagnostic test, sort of an enhanced MRI. The test came back positive, we showed it to the defense, and the offer went up about $300,000—based on that one test that cost us $1,500 (plus the cost of the neurologist). That's an example of knowing the right expert, hiring the right expert, having the right expert recommend the right test, and just like that, the defense was compelled to offer an extra $300,000 in the case. There are very few doctors in the state of Florida who do these DTIs, so the client had to travel down to south Florida for the DTI test. But we explained it to the client, we made it happen, and the result was a very positive result for the client. Without an advocate within our adversary system, no fair offer would have been made.

When not to litigate

Of course, the attorney also has to know when not to litigate. Low-impact cases are an example. It's very difficult to get a positive result from a low-impact case. Cases where there's no objective evidence of an injury are also very difficult to litigate successfully. In other words, where there's no positive MRI, or no positive X-rays with fractures, it's essentially the client telling the doctor that they are in pain. The doctor says, yes, there's a restriction on the range of motion, so therefore I give an impairment rating, but those are very difficult cases. Another factor that works against litigation is pre-existing injuries. If a client has a lot of pre-existing problems in his neck, and there's a low-impact collision with no objective evidence of any worsening of that condition, it makes for a difficult situation to litigate.

There are multiple reasons not to litigate a bad case. One reason is that the lawyer will be throwing away money which could otherwise go to the client in the event of a settlement, even if the settlement is relatively modest. Another reason is the rules involving proposals for settlement in our state. In Florida, a client who brings a lawsuit that is not a strong suit, and for whatever reason loses the case, can end up owing the other side tens of thousands of dollars. That's a horrible result when the other side is the one that caused the injury. Now, there is insurance that can be purchased to protect a client against that situation, but overall it's always our goal to put the client in a better position as a result of coming to see us, not a worse position.

Litigating a difficult case and being successful against the odds can be very uplifting. The attorney must be able to evaluate the risks and advise the client appropriately. Once again, experience and knowledge are invaluable assets.

Points to Remember

1. A demand is usually made after maximum medical improvement is verified.

2. A quick demand can be done when policy limits are low and injuries are severe.

3. Litigation should be initiated immediately in certain cases.

Chapter 5: Evaluating the Case: What is it worth?

WHEN SOMEONE COMES IN to see me and I'm conducting an initial interview, clients frequently ask me what their case is worth. I explain to them the factors that the insurance companies consider in <u>evaluating a case</u>, or setting a monetary value on it.

In an auto case, for instance, we look at liability, we look at the nature of the impact, we look at the insurance coverage, and we look at objective evidence of injury. We also look at things like lost wages, pre-existing injuries, and subrogation issues.

The question of <u>liability</u> is really the question of who was at fault. In trial, the first question on the verdict form to be answered by the jury is whether the defendant was negligent. When we talk about liability, that's what we're talking about. Did the defendant fail to use reasonable care?

Here's an example. If I get a phone call and an individual tells me that they walked off the curb at a Wal-Mart and tripped and broke their ankle, I might ask, "Well, was the curb marked with yellow paint? Was it unduly slippery? Was it particularly high?" And the client says, "No, it's totally my fault, I just fell off the curb," I have to explain to the client that there's no case because there's no liability; there's no fault on the part of Wal-Mart.

But suppose someone calls and tells me they fell in a Wal-Mart or other store, and a cart had been left in an aisle. The cart was sticking out into the walkway, and for whatever reason the client didn't see it. Then there might be liability, because there was fault. That aisle should be unimpeded. So I would tell the client that there might be a case, because there's liability.

In an auto accident case, if someone calls me and says, "Yes, I was in an auto accident, but it was totally my fault," I'm going to say, "Well, I can answer your questions about what happens to medical bills under no-fault, but I can't really open a file for you if the accident was your fault. It needs to be the fault of the other driver."

Sometimes an individual can be ticketed and it's not his fault, or there may be comparative negligence. Just yesterday, I was in court because my client had gotten a ticket for making an illegal U-turn too close to an oncoming vehicle. Even though the other driver was a drunk driver who was arrested by the trooper who came to the scene, the trooper said my client shouldn't have turned because there was a car coming. What the trooper didn't know is that the car driven by the drunk driver was coming at an excessive rate of speed.

When we got the case, because the client's injuries were significant and there was a drunk driver on the other side, we hired an engineer to download the data control module—popularly known as the "black box"—of the defendant's vehicle. The black box showed that the defendant, in addition to being drunk, was driving at 75 miles an hour—in a 45 mile-an-hour zone. What the black box typically shows, and what it showed in this case, is the last five seconds before impact. It also shows when the brake is applied and when the driver takes his foot off the gas pedal. In this case, the drunk driver didn't apply the brakes until the last second before impact.

Even though my client had made the U-turn and this drunk driver was approaching from the rear, he was so impaired he didn't perceive that there was a vehicle in front of him. He was accelerating up until one second before impact. Then, one second before impact, he put his foot on the brake. The trooper didn't know that, because he didn't have access to the black box.

At the hearing on the traffic ticket, we brought the engineer into court and we elicited his testimony. He testified that his analysis showed that the defendant's vehicle was traveling at 75 miles an hour up to one second before the collision. I also asked him if he had been able to analyze how far back the defendant's vehicle was at the time my client made his U-turn. My client had been charged under a statute that says a U-turn is illegal if it's dangerous to other vehicles. So, the further back the drunk driver's vehicle was at the time my client made the U-turn, the more chance I would have of gaining an acquittal for my client on this charge.

The expert said that in his opinion, the distance was 675 feet to 850 feet. I said, "Well, that's between two and three football fields' distance when my client made his turn." He agreed. The end result was that the judge acquitted my client of the ticket, which helps with the personal injury case.

It doesn't directly apply because the judge's decision is not admissible in the subsequent civil case, but it would certainly be persuasive with the insurance company. That's an example of actually fighting the initial liability decision made by the police. It's not always determinative and it can be contested, but if for instance the drunk driver had tried to hire me, I would have said, "Well, your liability isn't very good. You were intoxicated and you ran into the rear end of the other car." It's important to analyze the liability and advise the client accordingly as to whether the liability is favorable or unfavorable in terms of the case.

The <u>impact</u> is another important variable. Generally speaking if there's little or no property damage, it makes the case harder. It's hard to convince a jury that an individual has received extensive physical injuries in a low-impact case. It's really challenging.

That doesn't mean a low-impact case is impossible. My office tried and won a low-impact case where the impact happened, as luck would have it, right in front of the Gainesville Police Department. It wasn't witnessed by the police, but several witnesses said they heard the crash. My wife made the decision to try the case because she liked the client and there was objective evidence of injury, which is another important factor to consider. In that case, there was a positive MRI. The client was a young woman and she suffered a herniated disc. So particularly when your client is relatively young, if there's objective evidence of injury and there's no other explanation for that injury, it makes the low-impact case stronger, as it does in any case.

In evaluating a case we're always looking for <u>objective evidence of injury</u>. Naturally if there's surgery in a case, the case is stronger because the defendant is liable for past and future medical expenses as well as past and future pain and suffering if it's a permanent injury. Objective evidence of injury is really important. We rely on the doctors and the diagnostic tests to produce that objective evidence of injury. If it's there, the case is stronger. If it's not there, the case is weaker. If there's no objective evidence of injury and it's a low-impact collision, it may not be a suitable case for litigation and we would advise the client accordingly.

Another really important factor is <u>insurance coverage</u>. What we look at first is the bodily injury liability coverage of the defendant, the individual who caused the accident. There may be two or three defendants. For instance, if an individual loans his car to a driver, both the driver's insurance and the owner's insurance are liable. If it's a work situation, the employer's insurance is liable. So the attorney has to know enough to get the right insurance policies—all of the applicable policies—and check for the liability insurance coverage on each policy.

Sometimes an individual defendant doesn't have bodily injury liability coverage. In most states, it's required, but unfortunately, in the state of Florida, it's not required. That means it's really important to check for what's called <u>uninsured or underinsured motorist coverage (UM)</u>. This is coverage which covers you if the defendant doesn't have enough coverage. This coverage isn't required either, but people often have it.

Along with the factors I've already discussed, we also look at <u>lost wages</u> in evaluating a case. Lost wages are an important component because they're on the verdict form. It's something that you can obtain damages for. These are economic damages, and whether or not there's a permanent injury, the defendant is liable for your lost wages. This would include past lost wages and future loss of earning capacity. Once again, it may be necessary to use experts to determine the past lost wages, past lost benefits, and future loss of earning capacity.

The amount of medical bills is a critical variable. Generally speaking, the higher the bills, the more treatment, the more valuable the case becomes. This is because the injured victim is responsible for the bills unless they have great insurance. If a defendant is liable, his insurance company can ultimately be held responsible. It is the lawyer's job to obtain the bills from every provider and advocate for compensation for bills reasonably certain to be paid in the future. In significant cases a life care planner may be utilized to assess future needs.

In a case currently in litigation, our client is now unable to work and we've hired an economist to look at the benefits package that he was receiving. We have to look at what the value of the 401(k) donations or benefits and the value of the lost insurance that he was getting from his employer. In this case, the economist is also sizing up the life care plan. She's totaling all the past and future medical expenses as well as the lost wages.

In some cases we hire a vocational expert. The role of the vocational expert is to determine what economic job opportunities are lost to the client who's been severely injured and translate that into dollars. An extreme example would be a baseball player who suffered a leg injury or arm injury and couldn't play anymore. Now maybe they can only act as a ticket-taker at a game. They're still able to work, but their work is limited.

In evaluating a case we always want to ask about pre-existing injuries. If the client is complaining about a neck injury and he's had a prior neck injury, I have to tell the client that the insurance company is going to use that as a defense to try and mitigate the damages. They will say that whatever injuries the client is complaining about now preexisted the accident. Sometimes that works for the insurance company; sometimes it doesn't. We can sometimes turn it against them in lower-impact cases by saying, "Hey, they were predisposed to an injury, but you really aggravated the situation."

In a case I just completed, my client was six weeks post-fusion surgery. He got rear-ended, and although the impact was slight, it was enough to re-aggravate the injury and he needed to have a second subsequent fusion. The defendant was liable and paid a substantial amount of money, but because it was a really low-impact case and there was a preexisting injury, the value of the case was lessened. So it's important to know about preexisting injuries because they can affect the value of the case.

Subrogation is one more factor that we have to consider. Subrogation refers to the fact that, after a settlement, you have to pay back certain kinds of insurance that have paid you benefits after an accident. The most common is health insurance. For example if an individual has Blue Cross and Blue Cross paid $30,000 in medical bills, state law as well as the contract with Blue Cross requires us to pay Blue Cross back after the case is settled.

What we need to do is find out what the health insurance has paid. If the health insurer has a right of subrogation—and this also applies to things like disability insurance and other benefits an individual may receive after an accident—we have to determine what has to be paid back. This doesn't apply to PIP insurance, which is the state-required insurance for any driver. You don't have to pay them back, but you do have to pay back the health insurance. We frequently negotiate with those companies because every dollar that we save on a payback to the health insurance company is an extra dollar in the client's pocket.

It's very strange, but there is no uniform law on subrogation. Each specific health insurance policy has to be individually analyzed to determine the nature and extent of the subrogation. There is a federal law called the Employee Retirement Income Security Act (ERISA) that covers employee benefit plans, and if an insurance policy is an ERISA policy, it's harder to negotiate the subrogation than if it is not an ERISA policy. Subrogation can be a very complicated subject and I will sometimes even talk with other expert attorneys to get their opinions about the nature of the subrogation and what we can do about lessening the payment to the insurance company.

So you can see from this that the client's first question about what their case is worth is not as simple as they might expect. In evaluating a case we're looking at a whole universe of factors. Although I may be able to make a preliminary evaluation, it's really hard to give the client an exact figure when you first meet with them. At that point you can't know for sure how a lot of these factors are going to play out. When a client first comes in for an appointment, I may be able to determine the existence of an insurance policy, but I may not know the exact amount. I may be able to determine the liability if I get an accident report. I can often assess the impact because the client will usually have pictures taken on their cell phone.

What I don't know right off the bat is what's going to happen in the treatment process. Is there going to be objective evidence of injury? Of course sometimes I'll meet with people in hospitals and it's very obvious there's been a very serious injury, and at that point I can tell them "Your case is worth hundreds of thousands of dollars depending on the insurance coverage." But most of the time when I see someone for the first time in my office, I don't know how their injuries are going to resolve. I do know that we will advocate for the best possible result.

Points to Remember

1. Liability (Fault)

2. Coverage

3. Objective Evidence of Injury

4. Economic Impact

5. Social and Family Impact

6. Subrogation

Chapter 6: Litigation and Discovery

AFTER A LAWSUIT is filed, the discovery portion of a case begins. By discovery, we mean the ability of both sides in a civil case to obtain documents, take depositions, procure records, and basically gather all of the information pertinent to the case.

The discovery phase typically lasts until close to the pretrial conference, when you meet with the judge in the weeks before the trial. Discovery can take a long time; in some cases it literally lasts for years. Once the case is set for trial, the judge issues an order saying that the discovery has the stop on a given day.

The discovery process can be very detailed and include a whole variety of elements. Let's talk about some of the common discovery tools.

Tools of discovery

The process usually starts with interrogatories (see Exhibit C), which are written questions from each side to the other. The questions are pretty standard things like: What is your name and address? Have you ever been known by any other name? How did the accident happen? For auto accidents there's a standard list set forth by the Supreme Court of

Florida. And without special order of the court, you can only go up to 30 written questions.

Usually the attorney will prepare the interrogatories and send a copy to the client for review and signature, keeping in mind that the interrogatory is a sworn document.

The most critical questions concern how the accident happened, and any prior medical history that an individual has. The response to the interrogatories can lead into the next category of discovery, which is a request for production. A request for production is one side or another asking the attorney to produce paperwork.

For example, if the case involves an accident with a large truck, the plaintiff's attorney might issue a request for production seeking the truck driver's qualifications file, to see if it is in compliance with the standards required by the Federal Motor Carrier Safety Regulations (FMCSR). The defendant's attorney might request production of the plaintiff's tax records, if the plaintiff is claiming some sort of lost wages. And the plaintiff may respond by objecting to the request. Either party can object to the request for production, on various grounds. They may say that a request is overbroad and needs to be narrowed, or they may say that the records requested contain confidential information and need to be redacted.

Once a lawsuit is filed, the parties also have the ability to issue subpoenas to third parties for the production of documents. For instance, if the interrogatories state that a plaintiff saw doctors X, Y, and Z, during the past 10 years, the defense then has the power to issue subpoenas to X, Y, and Z doctors and have them produce all the medical records. Both sides will index the records, read them over carefully, and try to correlate those records with the medical records of the treating physician, which they have also subpoenaed. When depositions are taken, if a witness says something which is contrary to some of this documentation, their testimony can be impeached, or challenged, because it conflicts with the evidence already obtained.

Another common discovery tool is a <u>request for admission</u>. A request for admission allows either party to give the opposing attorney a list of statements for which they are seeking admission. The plaintiff's attorney might send to the defendant statements like: (1) "On this date you were driving a 1998 blue Chevrolet. (2) At this time and place you crashed into the rear of the plaintiff's vehicle. (3) The plaintiff did nothing to contribute to this accident. (4) The total fault of the accident lies with you, the defendant." The lawyer who receives this request for admission must respond within a specific time period with either an admission or a denial. If a statement is admitted, then it can be published at trial for the jury as a fact that doesn't need to be proven at trial. If the statement is denied, then it does need to be proved.

Over the years, technology has added even more elements to our discovery process. Cell phone records and social media have become really important.

In accident cases, it's always important to obtain the phone number and the provider for the opposing driver. They will do the same for the plaintiff if he's been driving, and then the phone records can be subpoenaed. The idea is to see if either party was on the phone at the time of the crash. Although it is not illegal in the state of Florida to be on the phone while driving, as it is in some states, it can be evidence for the jury to consider in determining the negligence of the driver who is on the phone.

Social media records are also commonly utilized in discovery. Just this week, my wife was negotiating a case with the defense. According to his medical doctors, our client was injured, but the defense has downloaded a bunch of photos from the client's Facebook page. The photos show him playing volleyball at the beach, and lifting heavy objects, and doing other things that cast doubt on his claim of serious injury. Now it's entirely possible that when that client got home from the beach, he had to lay down and rest for hours, and take pain medication, and he's really hurting, but that's not what the photographs show. The photographs show a smiling person having fun on the beach.

As attorneys for the plaintiff, the more explaining we have to do, the more difficult our job becomes. We tell our clients that they need to be aware that their Facebook accounts and other social media will be scrutinized, and they shouldn't post compromising material. It's important for clients to understand that their lives are going to be scrutinized by the defense. That's the job of the defense, to dig up as many inconsistencies as possible.

In one recent trial, the defense tried to make a big deal out of the fact that the plaintiff, our client, told one doctor that he was traveling at 10 miles an hour when he was hit by the bus, and told another doctor that it was 20 miles an hour when he was hit by the bus. Our client didn't know exactly how fast he was traveling, and the person who was interviewing him didn't warn him that he needed to be absolutely sure about what he said.

Your comments can be used against you down the road, and if there's any inconsistency in your account to the doctors, a jury can be told that they should disregard your testimony.

It's one of those things that people need to be careful about, because the medical records will be produced in discovery and any small slip-ups or inconsistencies can be used against them in the trial.

It doesn't have to be a deliberate attempt to deceive; it can be simple forgetfulness. Let me give you an example. Years ago, I was carrying a ladder and I slipped, fracturing a rib. Several years later, I was talking with someone about some sort of injury, and the question of broken ribs came up and I said, "Well, I've never broken a rib." And my wife reminded me, "Oh, yes you did, it was four years ago when you were carrying that ladder."

When she said that, it all came back to me. I wasn't deliberately trying to deceive anyone, I had just forgotten. In the day-to-day hustle and bustle of life, we don't remember every detail of every event with pinpoint accuracy. And there are some things that we maybe want to forget. But if the case goes to trial, that kind of forgetfulness will be utilized by opposing counsel to try to convince a jury that the witness, whether plaintiff or defense, is not telling the truth. Sometimes that's true. Sometimes people do lie; people do say things that aren't true. It's up to the lawyer to try and convince a jury, or convince a judge, whether a discrepancy is simple forgetfulness or a deliberate attempt to deceive.

Depositions

Depositions are where the discovery process comes to life. The other tools of discovery—the requests for production, the interrogatories, the requests for admissions, subpoenas of documents—are essentially the attorneys all shuffling paper back and forth. It can be very important paper that's shuffled, and the attorney needs the experience and skill to know what they should be requesting and what they should be looking for, but a deposition is a live process. In a deposition, the witness is asked questions and his answers are recorded by a court reporter for future potential use at trial or for discovery purposes.

We work with our clients to help them prepare for deposition. It's important to prepare a client for deposition, particularly since more and more depositions are put on video. The advantage of that is you can then play the video to the jury.

The rules of civil procedure in the state of Florida provide that depositions can only be shown to the jury under certain circumstances. Expert depositions can be shown under almost any circumstances. Depositions of a party can be shown under any circumstances. So the video deposition of a critical witness, or an expert witness, or a party can often be utilized in trial and shown to the jury. We want our clients to look good, and sound good, and be accurate.

There are different ways of preparing a client for deposition. Written materials can be sent to the client, particularly the interrogatories because those are the framework by which the defense devises the deposition questions.

The interrogatories are wide ranging about the client's past, their medical history, and what the client believes happened in the crash. So the defense attorney or opposing attorney will have those interrogatory questions, and will devise the deposition questions accordingly. When they take our client's deposition they will frequently have the medical records that they have subpoenaed, so they may go back five years and say, "What did you tell the emergency room doctors when you were in an accident in New Jersey in 2005?" Well, most people aren't going to remember exactly what they told an emergency room doctor 10 or 15 years ago about what was hurting them way back then.

That's why the client needs to be prepared and told what kind of questions to anticipate. But the overriding thing I tell my clients is to tell the truth. I tell them, "You can't be hurt if you're truthful." We certainly advise our clients not to elaborate on any particular issue, in other words, to just answer the question and then stop. We prepare them as best we can, but you never know until you're in the deposition how your client is going to do. You may have someone who's not well-educated but is a really good witness. They listen to the question, they process it, and they answer the question. They don't volunteer additional information; they keep their answers short and sweet.

You can also have someone who is actually very intelligent and articulate, but who likes to hear himself talk. They like to blabber on. That individual is usually not a good client in the deposition room. Their deposition is going to be longer, they're going to give the defense more material, and it could it turn out to be a long drawn-out process. I always want my client's deposition to be as short as possible. It is stressful for them, because it's not something they're used to. No one, in their day-to-day life, is used to going into a room, sitting in a table, perhaps being photographed by a video camera, being sworn to tell the truth, and then being asked a bunch of questions, many of which may seem to them irrelevant or insulting and totally unnecessary.

The defense strategy usually includes asking a lot of questions about background: "Where did you live? What was that address? Where did you live before that? Where did you work? How much money were you making at that job?" After 40 minutes of that, the client gets tired, and when the client gets a little tired, the defense will then switch to the actual facts of the case, which are far more important. The law allows the defense to cast a fairly wide net in terms of what may be discoverable, and I've found more often than not that objecting to stupid or unnecessary defense questions just raises the hackles of the defense attorney and prolongs the deposition. So as long as the questions aren't completely insulting, I will allow them to be asked and try to facilitate a fairly quick resolution to the deposition rather than object to every third question which some attorneys do.

I can think of some examples of really abusive deposition questioning, though. One instance that comes to mind was a wrongful death case. My client was a surviving parent of a young lady who had been killed by a serial murderer. We were bringing a wrongful death lawsuit against the apartment complex where the murder took place, so the issue being contested was the liability of the apartment complex for the criminal attacks by a third party. The damages were pretty obvious, but the defense lawyer, who is no longer practicing law, was notorious for taking extended and lengthy depositions. He would have a series of lengthy questions that went something like this: "Well, when your daughter was in the sixth grade, who was your neighbor to the right of you?" The client would try to answer, and then he would go, "And at that time, who was your neighbor to the left of you?"

I'd heard this line of questions before from the same attorney. I considered it unnecessary and abusive in the context of a deposition, so in this case, I did object. I told the defense counsel and put it on the record that his questioning was abusive and unnecessary, that I was directing my client not to answer, and that the defense counsel could move on to another subject. The defense attorney did move on, and he should've been ashamed of himself for putting the parent of a murder victim through an extended deposition asking stupid, unnecessary, and to my mind, abusive questions. That's among the worst examples that I can think of, but it can be typical of the type of questions that defense lawyers ask. Lawyers working for insurance companies often dredge up a lot of unnecessary questions in the hope of wearing down a plaintiff so when they get to the critical questions the plaintiff may make a mistake.

I'm not saying that some of the questioning of the defense lawyers isn't valid or reasonable. I think it's important to see both sides to a question, but sometimes they go over the line in their questions and in the discovery process as a whole. When I'm doing a deposition, I usually have a particular aim or goal and prepared questions. I try to ask appropriate questions, get at the heart of the issue, and then be done with it. I try not to play games which can be counter-productive.

Sometimes you get a surprise in deposition. You expect pretty good testimony and instead you get great testimony. Not long ago I was deposing a driver who had rear-ended my client. The driver was subsequently charged with a DUI, so I said to him, "Well, were you impaired?" And he basically said, "Hell, yes, I was impaired." I asked him what he had ingested or done that rendered him impaired, and he said, "Well, first I smoked some pot that morning. Then a little later on I went to my coworker's house and we drank a six-pack of beer. Then we snorted a bunch of cocaine." Whoa! This was pretty surprising testimony, and will result in a punitive damage claim.

The witness was remorseful and he told the truth, and I did appreciate that, even if I was somewhat astounded about how forthcoming he was about the extent of his impairment.

I got some great admissions in the deposition, and at the end of the deposition the defense said, "Oh, we're going to stipulate to liability." They hadn't stipulated to liability before. Not only had the defense denied liability, they also asserted an <u>affirmative defense</u>, saying the accident was my client's fault. So I also asked this witness whether my client had done anything wrong in her driving, and he said no, that she didn't do anything wrong, he was impaired and he slammed into her as she was making a left turn.

The end result of the discovery process and the depositions can make it possible for an attorney to file a motion for <u>summary judgment</u>. This may eliminate some of the issues in the case, making the case simpler and easier and putting more pressure on the other side.

Points to Remember

1. Preparation is key.

2. Familiarity with medical history is important.

3. Ongoing communication with attorney is essential.

4. Be absolutely truthful at deposition.

Chapter 7: Hiring Experts

THE RIGHT EXPERT can make or break a case, so let's talk a bit about experts and what kind of experts we need. It's really important for plaintiffs' lawyers to know which experts to hire, to have the resources to hire those experts, and then to know what to do with the expert's report or testimony once they get it. It works both ways. You have to be able to cross-examine the defense expert and you have to hire, prepare, and be ready to defend your own expert.

Case Study: Black box download

Let me give you a couple of examples. In the chapter discussing case evaluation I mentioned a recent car accident in which both drivers were ticketed. The opposing driver was charged with DUI, but the trooper maintained that our client made an illegal U-turn thereby contributing to the accident. Our client's injuries were serious and the policy limits were significant, so we decided we needed to hire an accident reconstruction engineer. An accident reconstruction engineer is an expert who is experienced in analyzing all of the information relating to an accident to determine exactly what happened and how. In this case the engineer not only examined the scene of the accident, he also downloaded the seatbelt control module—also known as the black box—from the defendant's car. We got permission from the defense to do that.

As I explained in the earlier chapter, we were able to use this expert's findings in contesting our client's traffic ticket. Our client did not want to pay the traffic ticket because he felt that he was not at fault, and we thought this would be worthwhile to do, even though the determination of a judge at a traffic hearing is typically not admissible in a subsequent civil lawsuit.

With the engineer's testimony, we were able to argue to the county judge who was hearing the case that the accident really wasn't our client's fault and we were able to get the ticket dismissed.

Will that make a giant difference in a subsequent civil case against the drunk driver, who was driving a company truck when he struck our client? The determination of the county judge won't matter because that's inadmissible, but the fact that the drunk driver was going at 75 miles an hour in a 45 mile-an-hour zone is certainly significant, as is the fact that he was accelerating right up until impact. He literally ran his car right into the rear of our client's car.

Case Study: Biomedical engineer

Engineers can do more than reconstruct accidents. In Chapter 2 I described the case of Mr. Davis, whose case recently concluded with a $438,000 verdict after we rejected a $20,000 offer. In his case my wife hired a biomedical engineer whose expert testimony made all the difference.

In Mr. Davis's case, the injuries weren't obvious. Initially it looked like a whiplash case, but then gradually the injuries grew worse and Mr. Davis ended up having a carpal tunnel release and an ulnar nerve release. He had been in two relatively low-impact collisions within a few months. There was very little visible property damage in the first accident, but he had a trailer hitch, and there was a small dent in the trailer hitch. We know from prior cases and from talking to experts that when you have a trailer hitch, which is bolted to the frame of the car, any impact bypasses the car's energy-absorbing bumpers. The energies of the impact are transmitted directly to the frame, and to the occupants of the car, who are sitting on the frame. Although the visible property damage in his case was very minor, Mr. Davis—a small business owner in his fifties—was claiming a permanent injury based on the medical records.

I was considering bringing in the body shop technicians to talk about the dent in the trailer hitch, but when my wife Cherie took over the case, she hired a biomedical engineer from Tallahassee. We ended up paying him about $20,000 dollars. We actually took the trailer hitch out of the body of the pickup truck, brought it into court on a dolly, and showed it to the jury. Even though the dent was not large, this thing must have weighed a couple of hundred pounds. The engineer told the jury that yes, from a scientific point of view—even though the dent in the trailer hitch was small—the impact carried enough force to cause nerve damage in the arms, which resulted in our client needing the carpal tunnel and the ulnar nerve release surgeries.

The insurance company had initially offered only $5,000 for each of the two incidents, for a total of $10,000. When the case went to trial, the jury brought back a verdict of $438,000. That engineer's expert testimony was critical to that outcome. And we just received a ruling that in addition to the $438,000 verdict, we're entitled to another $225,000 in attorneys' fees because the defense was unreasonable in turning down our initial proposal for settlement. The point is Cherie was willing to spend the $20,000 for the expert, and choosing the right expert made all the difference.

Case Study: Replacing incompetent expert

Experts have done some great work for us in innumerable cases, but it is important to hire the right expert. One of my earliest product liability cases involved a device called a climbing tree stand. My client was a retired fireman. He loved to hunt, and he moved up to North Central Florida. He bought a tree stand from a small company. A tree stand is a device that a hunter puts up in a tree, to aid in spotting game. You sit there on the tree stand and you wait for the deer or other animal to come along. The stand was made of metal—this one was made out of steel—and the idea was that you could use it to slowly climb up the trunk of the tree. When you got to a sufficient height, then you would stabilize it and settle in to wait for the game to appear.

Unfortunately this climbing tree stand was defectively designed. It collapsed under pressure, and it ended up holding my client sort of upside down in a position that put a lot of pressure on various limbs causing nerve damage. As a result, my client, who was just going to enjoy his retirement, was rendered an incomplete quadriplegic as a result of this defective product.

I hired an expert, a former professor of engineering and metallurgy at the University of Florida, to examine the tree stand and give me an opinion. The defense attorney took his deposition. I was really dismayed by this expert's deposition. His qualifications were very good, but it seemed to me that he hadn't spent much time thinking through his analysis. His deposition was not helpful, and he even came to the deposition wearing old, beat-up clothes. He was just really inappropriate. As a result, the defense, despite catastrophic injuries, and a one million dollar insurance policy, made a minimal offer of barely six figures. That wasn't even enough to cover the medical bills.

The medical bills were paid by Medicare and a Medicare supplement, but they had a right of subrogation. We had to pay them back. I was extremely upset with the performance of this particular expert, who had come highly recommended. I liked and admired our client, who was a fantastic individual and I wanted to do the best I could for him. I was determined to find a better expert and see if we could revisit the liability issue. I ended up going to Tallahassee and hiring a very experienced professional engineer, who had a completely different take on the case. When he examined the tree stand, he explained to me why it was defective, and was even able to come up with an alternative design that would have prevented it from collapsing. The defense counsel took his deposition, and within two or three weeks after that deposition, the defendants paid their policy limit of $1 million in the case.

They paid, of course, because the accident was catastrophic, but the difference between their five-figure offer and their seven-figure offer was the fact that we had a really good expert who could explain why they were liable. Obviously, I never used that first expert again and would not recommend him. That's the difference that hiring the right expert can give you in a case.

Points to Remember

1. Attorney must have litigation experience.

2. Correct expert(s) must be hired.

3. Attorney must have ability to do discovery, depositions, and cross-examination.

4. Attorney must have financial resources to do the job.

Chapter 8: More Truths about Insurance Companies

INSURANCE COMPANIES and insurance coverage play a big role in any personal injury case, but being involved in an accident is a bad way to learn about insurance issues. There are a few basic things you should know about insurance; being prepared can help you avoid unpleasant surprises if you do find yourself involved in an accident.

I don't want to make a blanket statement that insurance companies are unfair, but the fact of the matter is that insurance companies are trying to make a profit. They're trying to save money, and they don't do that by paying out on claims. So even though you buy insurance to protect yourself, when a claim happens you are in an adversarial relationship with either your own insurance company or the insurance company for the other party, also known as the tortfeasor, or the defendant, or the wrongdoer.

Because you're in an adversarial relationship, it's really important to get legal advice so that you can at least have some chance of standing up to these giant corporations. They have millions of dollars' worth of resources and people who are trained to, in my opinion, undervalue cases.

Now, it is important to note that this opinion is coming from a plaintiff's lawyer. I am not an unbiased individual. I typically represent people who are injured and who have been through a traumatic situation, but I will try to be objective in giving you my opinions based on my years of experience.

But the truth is that it's in the DNA of insurance companies to maximize their profits, and the best way to maximize their profits is at the expense of people who have been injured and who are making claims against them. If the company can save money on paying out claims, they make more money for the insurance company and its shareholders. So the training, the job, and the whole thrust of their existence is to save money whenever possible.

I should note that there are a lot of state and federal regulations in place to try to make insurance companies do the right thing. Florida statutes passed by the legislature say specifically that insurance companies must treat people fairly. How do you enforce such a statute? You can only enforce a statute if the individual being treated unfairly has an attorney who can bring the situation to the attention of an impartial tribunal, meaning a judge or a jury. The state really doesn't do anything to enforce that law that an insurance company must treat somebody fairly.

In my practice, every day I see examples of insurance companies treating claimants unfairly. The truth is that a certain amount of unfairness is built into the system: Insurance companies almost always negotiate, and when they do they start off with a low-ball offer. You could call it an unrealistic offer, but what they're trying to do is settle the cases for less than they are worth.

The fact is, in virtually every case they start with an offer lower than the one we eventually obtain. That's a pretty good indication that their starting offer is unfair.

Beware of a quick settlement

Many insurance companies will try and settle cases right away. A person has been in an accident, they've been to the hospital, they've been released, and they have injuries. The insurance companies will approach them and say, "Well, I'm very sorry that you've been injured, but we're willing to settle this case now. It'll be so much easier than hiring a lawyer and negotiating with us. We're willing to pay you X amount of money if you sign a release right now."

Of course what the insurance company is trying to do is cut off its exposure by settling the case before the client has a chance to get the injury evaluated. They know that very often it takes some time for the full extent of the injuries to be determined by a physician or by an individual. What they want to do is strike while the iron is hot, take advantage of an individual who may really need money, and pay less than the case is worth.

Avoid the spin

The insurance company is often willing to make arguments that they know are incorrect. If a fact can be misinterpreted to the claimant's detriment, that's what they will do. For example, if it takes you a week to make an appointment with a doctor, the insurance company will spin that as a gap in treatment. They will say that you must not have been hurt because you didn't see a doctor right away. On the other hand, if you have seen a doctor and had many appointments, they will say that they shouldn't have to pay because you are over-treating. They get you either way.

If there was some sort of preexisting injury, they will always try and blame the preexisting injury. And the doctors hired by insurance companies will almost always classify an injury as preexisting or as a soft-tissue injury that should be better in a few weeks.

Here's a typical situation. An individual has been in a crash, and doesn't have a lawyer, so an insurance company sends him to the company's doctor. This doctor believes that whiplash injuries are always better in eight weeks. So no matter how severe the injury, even if tests later show that there was a herniated disk, that there was ligamentous injury or some other objective indication of injury, the insurance companies will cut off benefits because their own doctor doesn't believe that an individual can continue to hurt after eight weeks.

I have a similar situation in a case right now. There's a mild traumatic brain injury. The insurance company hired a neuropsychologist to conduct an examination of my client, and her conclusion, which flies in the face of numerous medical articles, journals, and peer-reviewed studies, is that mild traumatic brain injuries can't be chronic. She believes they can't be permanent, so she thinks the client must be either making it up, or imagining it, or is suffering from some other condition like depression, but he can't have a brain injury.

Radiologists are among the worst offenders. There are a number of radiologists in the state of Florida who get paid millions of dollars by insurance companies. It's very unfortunate because it gives an appearance that testimony can be bought, particularly when there's a long-term relationship between the insurance companies and the physicians.

Watch out for offer by algorithm

A few years ago, plaintiff's attorneys became aware that several insurance companies had essentially installed rigged computer programs. For certain types of cases, decisions were not being made by individual adjusters, but by an insurance software program. The data inputted into the insurance program would be the extent of the property damage, considerations on liability, the number of medical treatments, and boom!—out would pop a proposed settlement amount. The adjusters were told they couldn't go above this particular settlement range. Of course, it was easy enough for the insurance companies just to set very low ranges for the given parameters that were inputted into the computers.

Now, there are different things that attorneys can do to try to influence the offers that are made, but the bottom line is the insurance companies set up these computer programs to save money, to cut costs on their evaluation of cases, and to cut costs on settlements. The claimant gets told, "Hey, this is all we can do and it's based in part on our computer evaluation and you can take it or leave it." Unless an individual is willing to push the insurance company, or is willing to litigate, these rigged computers and unfair claims practices will continue.

How insurance has changed

Years ago, it was a little different. When I first started doing this kind of work, large national insurance companies had local offices with local claims adjusters. The claims adjusters got to know the attorneys and the attorneys got to know the claims adjusters. The adjusters would visit with us and talk with us about the case. They would get a much better sense of what the case was about, what our clients were about, and objective indications of what the case was worth.

To save money, the insurance companies changed their business model from local offices to centralized offices. What that means is that none of the adjusters really know the attorneys. It's much more impersonal, and makes it easier for the insurance companies to tell their adjusters, "You're just going to follow this model, and it doesn't matter what the attorneys say."

I really think it was different when the adjusters could meet with us, look us in the eye, talk the case over, and come up with a fair evaluation. It seems as though the power to make decisions on cases has been taken away from individuals. The power is now ensconced in far-off offices in far-off cities, and so divorced from the reality of what has happened to our clients after an injury.

Mediation

Insurance company centralization has affected the mediation process as well. Every litigation case is ordered to mediation prior to trial, and overall, mediation is a good idea and a good process. Mediation is a settlement conference presided over by an independent third party. The mediator is usually a lawyer or a former judge who has taken courses and gotten certified by the Supreme Court of Florida as a mediator. The idea is that both parties go to the mediation with the ability and the authority to settle the case. You're there with your client, a representative of the insurance company is usually there with their attorney, and you meet in a room with the mediator. Each side gives a short presentation, and then typically the parties separate and the mediators go back and forth between the rooms trying to convince the plaintiff that their position is unreasonable and they ought to go lower, and the defense that their position is unreasonable and they ought to go higher.

It is theoretically required that the insurance company representative have full settlement authority. The problem is they don't. The way it really works at mediation is that before the parties even get to the mediation, the insurance company has evaluated the case and put a number on it. The actual insurance company representative at the mediation often has very little power.

The idea is that mediation brings back the sort of personal experience that has been lost with the centralization of the insurance companies. In the mediation, an insurance company representative and attorney can meet with the plaintiff, look him or her in the eye, evaluate the plaintiff's attorney, and together with the mediator come to a fair resolution of the case. But it's not fair if the individual who is sent to the mediation by the insurance company has no power. If the insurance company position has already been determined, it's really not a fair mediation. It's just the plaintiff trying to get the best number out of the defendant and the mediator trying to get the defendant to their top number as efficiently as possible.

It's really unfortunate when insurance companies don't mediate in good faith. If there is a good faith offer on the table at mediation, the attorney can explain to the client the positives and the negatives of going to trial, and the fact that a case can be lost. But if there's no good faith offer, it's pointless to urge the client to settle the case because there's no real basis to settle and the next step is to go to trial.

It's particularly irritating when the defense is mediating in bad faith and then makes an offer later on as the trial approaches. But the insurance companies often don't make realistic offers at mediation.

Good and bad lawyers

I like most of the lawyers I come in contact with. I've been coming in contact with attorneys for 40 years, and a lot of times these attorneys are my adversaries. When I was a public defender, I liked most of the attorneys in my office, I thought they were a great group and highly skilled individuals and extremely dedicated. Opposing me were the state attorneys. It is not a coincidence that I urged my daughter to join the state attorney's office after law school. In part, my decision was made easy because I really liked the chief assistant in the state attorney's office, who had sort of grown up as a young criminal lawyer with me. She was my opposite number when I was in the public defender's office. Naturally there were some state attorneys I didn't like, but often I was friends with the lawyers.

The same thing holds true for the personal injury work that I'm doing now. I often enjoy working with opposing counsel. They're fair, they're honest, they do their job, and when they do their job skillfully I can admire the legal work they do such as their ability in court with cross examinations or direct examinations. However, a significant number of the civil insurance defense bar seem to be motivated by financial considerations. They're paid at an hourly rate. As a result, they get more money if the case doesn't settle. I've had situations where I believe insurance defense lawyers, particularly if they are not house counsel but independently hired, are happier if a case doesn't settle. If the case goes to trial, they're going to make tens of thousands of dollars for themselves and their law firm, so they are not going out of their way to seek a resolution.

It's not frivolous lawsuits; it's frivolous defenses

When we're picking juries, prospective jurors frequently talk about frivolous lawsuits. This is because of the propaganda spread by the insurance companies. Defense lawyers would like to tell you all about frivolous lawsuits brought by plaintiffs. Nothing could be further from the truth. The way it works in contingency fee cases is that we want to pursue cases that we think have a social benefit, or a benefit to our client, or will simply produce money, which really is the benefit to the client. We're not going to pursue a case that we think has no benefit, because it's a lot of wasted time. So the idea that attorneys bring cases they think are frivolous is simply wrong. I've never seen it.

The defense, on the other hand, has a motivation to raise frivolous defenses. The longer a case goes on, the more financial pressure is put on the plaintiff, and the more the defense lawyer gets paid. So with the way the system works, where the defense lawyers get paid by the hour, it makes much more sense for them to drag things out, slow things down, and prolong the litigation, to have the case go to trial. This doesn't happen on every case; it may not even happen in the majority of cases. But certainly it's not uncommon for the defense lawyers to take their time and stretch things out.

I've seen some defense lawyers conduct themselves in an unethical manner. I once had a situation where the defense hired a doctor to do independent medical examinations and then told the doctor to destroy some of the records when the examination didn't come out their way. Fortunately, it was easy to figure that one out when we took the doctor's deposition. If I hadn't deposed the doctor it might have been difficult, but we were able to bring the situation to the attention of the judge.

In one of my recent cases, we recently discovered that the defense withheld critical photographic evidence. We only found out about the existence of the photographs when we took the depositions of the defense experts. The defense had sent these photographs to their experts, but told us that the photographs didn't exist. Fortunately, we had the experts produce every scrap of evidence when we took their deposition pursuant to a subpoena, and so we learned about the photographs. These photographs proved that the comparative negligence defense was weak or non-existent. It was frivolous, but the defense thought they could get away with it. They didn't.

I've had cases where my clients were professionals, and the defense—for no other reason, I think, than to harass my client—said they wanted to take depositions of some of the plaintiff's clients. Of course, no professional person wants their clients bothered by the defense. Several clients felt that we should dismiss the lawsuit. So the defense tactic worked in that situation.

Delay can work to the advantage of the defense. The client will feel the pressure of having this case out there, maybe for years, and having to answer written questions, and having to have their deposition taken for hours by a defense lawyer. It can wear on a person and they'll just say they want it over with. Dragging the case out can work for the defense; there's no doubt about it.

The legislative factor: Legal payoffs

At the beginning of this chapter, I mentioned that the Florida legislature has put statutes in place that are intended to ensure that insurance companies treat customers and claimants fairly. But insurance companies have plenty of money, and because they have money, and they also have lobbyists—many more lobbyists than accident victims do. Plaintiffs' legal organizations do the best that they can, but it's all one-sided in the legislature. It's all on the side of the insurance companies.

A law was passed to say that if you're injured in an accident and you don't get treatment within 14 days, your benefits just go away. Your $10,000 in PIP just vanishes. And if you're in a crash and the doctor doesn't say that he's seeing you for an emergency medical condition, your $10,000 drops to $2,500. There are other provisions that benefit the insurance companies.

When people are called to serve on a jury, they are not told about the existence of insurance. A defendant can have a million dollar insurance policy, but if they look like a grandmother, a jury is going to feel sorry for them, and the plaintiff cannot mention the existence of liability insurance. There's something called the non-joinder statute, which prohibits us from joining a person's insurance company in a lawsuit unless it's, for instance, an uninsured motorist suit, or a first party suit for the cutting off of PIP benefits. There are statutes of limitations beyond which you cannot bring a claim.

These are all provisions that the insurance companies have passed, or gotten passed by the legislature, which stack the deck against accident victims. Fortunately the way it works with the contingent fee system, plaintiffs can hire really good lawyers to represent them without reaching into their pockets and spending money that they don't have.

These insurance companies really do have vast sums of money, and when little old Joe Schmoe comes up against an insurance company who has the power, how do you even up the odds? That's where we come in and try to help.

Points to Remember

1. Insurance companies will try to treat plaintiffs unfairly.

2. Frivolous defenses are common.

3. Legislation is paid for by industry lobbyists.

4. Having a competent trial lawyer can help level the playing field.

Chapter 9: Insurance 101— Understanding Your Policy

ONE OF THE BEST THINGS you can do to be prepared in the event of an accident is to understand your own insurance coverage. So let's talk a little bit about understanding your insurance policy and some of the common terms you'll see in any discussion of insurance.

Common insurance terms

The key to understanding your coverage is the <u>declarations page</u>, commonly called the <u>dec page (see Exhibit D in the Appendix)</u>. That's where you'll find a summary of all the basic information, including the types of coverage, the terms, the limits of that coverage. Unfortunately, the information on the dec page is not explained in plain language. What follows is a brief description of some common terms used in insurance policies.

<u>Personal Injury Protection (PIP)</u>—PIP coverage is mandatory in Florida. PIP covers 80 percent of medical bills and 60 percent of lost wages, up to $10,000. There are two caveats: you must be treated by a doctor within 14 days after a crash, or your coverage disappears, and a medical doctor has to say that it's an emergency condition, or your coverage

drops from $10,000 to $2,500. One of the nice things about PIP is there's no subrogation, meaning you don't have to pay it back if you eventually make a recovery from a third party. Another advantage is that you can choose your own doctor.

Property Damage Liability (PDL)—This is also mandatory coverage in Florida. If you get into an accident and damage someone else's property, whether it's a car or a fence or a building, your insurance company will pay on your behalf up to the amount of property damage coverage that you've purchased. It does not cover damage to your vehicle. The required minimum is $10,000 in PDL.

No-Fault—This is a commonly misunderstood term. People don't really know what it means. In the state of Florida, no-fault only applies to the medical bill coverage known as PIP. No matter who is at fault, your company pays. In other words, if you're in a crash, your insurance company will pay the first $10,000 of your medical bills (and 60 percent of lost wages) even if it's the other guy's fault.

Part of the no-fault statute involves permanent injuries. Essentially, what the legislature did was trade this no-fault coverage for a proposition that you can only make a claim for pain and suffering against a defendant if you have a permanent injury. So in order to pursue a claim against the other party we need to get reports from doctors documenting that an individual has sustained a permanent injury.

Medical Payments Coverage (MedPay)—This is an optional coverage in Florida. MedPay functions as a sort of supplement to the PIP coverage. The PIP covers 80 percent up to $10,000. People who purchase MedPay typically have it in amounts like $1,000, $2,000, or $10,000, and it supplements their PIP. In other words, if you have $12,000 in medical bills, the PIP will pay the first $10,000, and if you have $2,000 in MedPay that will pay the next $2,000.

MedPay is subject to subrogation, though, which means that if you make a recovery you against a third party, you have to pay your insurance company back the amount that they have extended to you, minus whatever the percentage of the attorney's fee is.

Bodily Injury Liability (BI)—In Florida, this is an optional coverage, and many drivers do not carry it, but it can be vitally important. As personal injury lawyers, we usually look first for BI coverage. If you hurt someone else through your negligence, a bodily injury liability claim can be made against you, but if you have BI coverage, you are protected. Your insurance company will provide counsel and they will pay up to the limit of your policy. One of the potential difficulties with that is that the insurance company calls all the shots if the case goes to litigation. If they want to save money and it results in your being sued, you can be dragged into a litigation process that you don't want to be in. You don't want to have to give a deposition, answer interrogatories, or appear in court, but the company can insist on it because they call the shots for any litigation under the BI policy.

On your policy's dec page, you will usually see BI limits expressed as two numbers, for example, 100/300. The first number is what any individual can be compensated. The second number is the total amount of coverage that's available. So on a 100/300 policy, if three people are hurt, the most any one person could receive from the insurance coverage would be $100,000, but the most any group of people could receive is $300,000. Suppose there are four people hurt. The most they could collect would still be $300,000.

Uninsured/Underinsured Motorist Coverage (UM)—Because Florida does not require BI coverage, many people do not include BI in their policy, and even those who do often do not have enough BI coverage. To help protect yourself, you can purchase UM coverage, which protects you from another's wrongdoing when they don't have enough coverage to pay the actual damages. For example, if an injury is serious and the defendant has only $10,000 in BI, your UM would be available on top of that. Typically you would first have to exhaust the BI coverage (if it exists), and then you can make a UM claim. UM can be stacking or not stacking. Stacking means that the policy coverages can be added together. Suppose you have three cars each with $100,000 in UM. If it's stacking coverage, you then have $300,000 worth of coverage. So, stacking is a good option if you're looking to increase your coverage.

Collision Coverage—This covers damage to your vehicle, and it almost always includes a deductible. If you are in an accident and it's your fault, your insurance company will pay for the damage to your vehicle. For example, if you have $5,000 worth of damage to your car and it gets taken to the body shop, and you have a $500 deductible on your collision policy, the insurance company will pay $4,500 and you will have to pay $500.

If the accident is someone else's fault, you can go through their PDL coverage. They will pay the whole thing, and they will reimburse you for a rental car while your car is in the shop, so it is financially advantageous to go through the other driver's collision coverage. But you should be aware that in this situation, the other party's insurance company is typically even more adversarial than your company. They will often not extend coverage to you until they get a copy of the accident report and take a statement from their insured. It can be easier and quicker to go through your own insurance company and then try to get your deductible back from the defendant's insurance company down the line if the other party caused the accident. So as far as collision is concerned, you have an option. You can go through your company if you have collision coverage, or you can go through the other party's insurance company. Your company may or may not compensate you for a rental car. The other party's company is supposed to pay for a rental or compensate you for loss of use of your vehicle.

If the damage to your vehicle is extensive, the insurance company may declare a total loss of the vehicle. Typically if the damage is 80 percent of the actual cash value of your vehicle, the vehicle will be totaled. Be aware that this is another point at which insurance companies can try to take advantage of individual victims. There are websites like Kelley Blue Book (www.kbb.com) and Edmunds (www.edmunds.com) where you can get a pretty good online appraisal of your vehicle. The insurance companies, however, frequently use their own proprietary databases or techniques, and their appraisal often come out 5 or 10 percent less than it really should be if you go by these more objective websites. Most people who have their vehicles damaged want replacements immediately; they don't want to wait a year while it's litigated whether the value of their car is $3,500 or $4,200. So this is an area in which insurance companies take advantage of individuals.

Umbrella Policy—Sometimes people purchase excess or umbrella policies over the BI or UM. These are actually a really good deal because they're very inexpensive, so I recommend them highly if they can be afforded. They add an additional layer of coverage for an individual when liability limits or UM limits have been exceeded. Usually insurance companies require substantial BI limits as a predicate for allowing the purchase of umbrella coverage.

That's basically an outline of an insurance policy. After an accident, we obtain the insurance policy and size it up. What we look for is either BI or UM because that enables us to make a claim on behalf of an injured client.

The myth of full coverage

In the state of Florida, you must have PDL coverage and PIP coverage. You don't have to have any of the other coverages. What I recommend is that you take a good look at your policy, see what your coverages are, and then depending on your financial situation, get the most coverage that you can afford. You want to have it balance out. I've seen policies where there's $100,000 in property damage, but no UM or no BI. It doesn't make sense to have one coverage so extraordinarily high but no protection for any of these other eventualities.

When I ask people about their insurance coverage, they'll frequently say, "I have full coverage."

They may think that because they have the required PIP and PDL, that they have "full coverage." In fact, they don't have full coverage; there's no such thing. They may have one or two types of coverage and they may have them in disproportionate numbers in either the property damage or the med pay, but they won't have the UM or they won't have the BI. I think it's critical for everyone to have some amount of BI and some amount of UM. You really don't need collision coverage if your vehicle is old and not worth much money. That's one that could be dispensed with. But the other coverages are critical. If you do have assets and you have some extra money, I would recommend you get an umbrella or excess policy on the BI. If you have even more assets, or you want to be really careful, I would recommend excess coverage on the UM.

I have gotten million dollar recoveries for people who have purchased large UM policies. As a matter of fact, in Mr. Davis's case, the one we just tried where the insurance company offered $20,000, and Cherie and Julie got a verdict of $438,000, that money will be coming to my client along with the $225,000 that was awarded for attorneys' fees. That money will be coming to our client because he purchased really good UM coverage. If he didn't have the UM coverage, he would be totally out of luck. I've had people who have sustained really serious injuries, including traumatic brain injuries, but there was no BI and no UM coverage. From a plaintiff's lawyer's point of view, there's not much that can be done to help them if there's no appropriate coverage.

So look at your own policy and make sure that you have good BI to protect you against an unfortunate mistake that you or a relative might make. Why do I say a relative? In choosing insurance, you have to consider vicarious liability. What that means is that if you lend your car to someone else and they get into a crash, their insurance would cover, but your insurance would be primary. In the state of Florida, the owner's insurance is primary. So you need to be aware that you can be vicariously liable if you loan your car out. You just want to protect yourself. If you have a child who reaches the age of 18 and has their own car, you may want to make sure the car is titled in just their name and put them on a separate policy because you are exposed for their mistakes, and statistics show that younger drivers make more mistakes than older drivers do. Just think about protecting yourself. Don't have a car listed in your name if someone else is the actual owner; it should be put in their name. Let them get their own policy. Make sure that your own coverage is adequate and not just limited to one or two areas.

Other types of insurance

When an individual has been in an accident, they often need to look at their complete insurance package, and not just their auto insurance. If they can't work, they may have a disability policy that needs to be engaged. They could add short-term disability or long-term disability, or they may need help with an application for long-term or short-term disability. They should talk to an attorney about this if there's any question about it. There may also be an interaction between workers' comp coverage and their auto insurance.

When someone comes to me with an on-the-job injury they incurred in their motor vehicle, they have an option of going through their workers' comp coverage or going through the PIP coverage of their auto insurance. Sometimes an individual will be referred to a doctor in workers' comp, but we would rather they see a doctor through their PIP because then they get to choose their own doctor. The problem is that the doctors who treat worker's comp patients are typically more conservative and geared to minimizing the injury so that the individual returns to work as soon as possible.

That's why the comp carriers use them for referrals, so that the company can minimize the benefits it needs to pay out.

Let me give you an example of a workers' comp case. My client—we'll call her Mrs. Regan—was a visiting nurse. She would travel around to houses to do in-home care. She got into an accident. The workers' comp carrier sent her to a doctor, who said, "You have symptoms of a herniated disc. You need an MRI." But the comp carrier said no, they didn't want to order an MRI. They proposed that Mrs. Regan just do physical therapy without the MRI.

A few more days went by, and Mrs. Regan was still having advancing neurological symptoms. When you have a herniated disc in your low back, if it's pressing on a nerve, it's pretty clear that you have a serious problem. You lose control of your walking ability on that leg because the nerve in the low back runs down the leg. The sciatic nerve controls a lot of function in the leg, and it's extremely painful. So she went back to the comp doctor, who said, again, "We need an MRI. We need a surgical consult. You need to see a neurosurgeon." They finally sent her to the neurosurgeon and ordered the MRI, which showed a herniated disc. The neurosurgeon recommended surgery, but the comp carrier wanted more physical therapy instead.

It got to the point where the client was losing control of her bladder, which is a clear sign of nerve damage. And finally, after several weeks of this, we were able to persuade the comp carrier to send her to a neurosurgeon who recommended immediate emergency surgery for her. That's not something that happens all the time, but just generally, the comp doctors are more conservative. The trouble is they're serving two masters: One is the insurance company and one is the patient. And it's never good when the doctors are not 100 percent dedicated to the wellbeing of the patient.

Normally doctors follow the Hippocratic Oath. They do no harm. They do their best for the patient. When an insurance company hires the doctor, particularly in a one-time compulsory medical evaluation, there is no doctor-patient relationship, and that's a critical difference. That's why doctors who are being paid by the insurance companies frequently slant their testimony to benefit their employers.

One last note

For the record: All of the recommendations in this chapter are general principles. I am a lawyer, not an insurance agent, and you should always ask your insurance agent about what coverage is best for you.

Points to Remember

1. Bodily Injury (BI)—Optional coverage on behalf of at-fault driver

2. Uninsured Motorist (UM)—Optional protection in case defendant has little or no BI

3. Personal Injury Protection (PIP)—Required "no fault" coverage for your medical bills

4. Umbrella or excess coverage is a great optional coverage to protect you further.

Chapter 10: Auto Accidents

THE MOST COMMON TYPE of personal injury case we see is an auto accident. That's not surprising, of course, because everyone uses cars for transportation and inevitably there are people who are careless with their driving and cause preventable collisions.

This category includes accidents between cars and pedestrians, cars and bicyclists, cars and cars, and cars and trucks—we see all of these in our office. Impacts vary from very slight to quite severe. We have to counsel individuals who come to us after an accident. Frequently, they're hurting; they don't know what to do or where to go; they don't know who to talk to. Many of them don't even know that they're supposed to notify their insurance company.

Sometimes people call us from the scene of the accident, and we have to tell them to call 911 and report it to the police, because we want there to be a police report. Obviously, the first priority should be to request emergency medical treatment if warranted. You'd be surprised at how some people don't call the police; they just exchange cards with the other driver and leave.

At the scene

On the scene of an accident, even if it seems to be a minor incident, it's always a good idea to call the police. In fact, it's required by law under a lot of circumstances; certainly, if there's an injury, it's required. You should not leave the scene of an accident without notifying the police.

Seek medical attention: If there's doubt about how you're feeling, seek medical attention as quickly as possible. If you really think you are hurt, you should go to an emergency room.

The problem with going to an emergency room, of course, is that there are sometimes long waits, and the bills are just outrageous. We're now seeing bills of $20-$30,000 for an emergency room visit, with a few CAT scans, and they don't really even treat you. They are looking for life-threatening injuries or broken bones. So they take a few x-rays, or a CAT scan, and you're done.

In Florida, you have typically $10,000 in PIP coverage, as we discussed in the last chapter. You don't want to use it all up at the emergency room, but you may have no choice. It's going to be used up at the emergency room, if you have to go there. Alternatives to the emergency room are urgent care centers or a visit to your primary care doctor. If there is any question about serious injury go to the emergency room.

Take photos: Of course, the first thing is always to check for injuries. Assuming that you are able to do so, then take photographs. Almost everyone carries a cell phone with a camera. Use it to take a range of photos. Sometimes, we get photographs of the damage, but they're so close in that we can't even tell what part of the vehicle it is, or which vehicle it is.

What you want to do is take a whole range of photographs, including close-ups of the damage, but then from further away and from different angles, so we can see where the damage is and how it all fits together. You want pictures of the other vehicle as well.

The defense will frequently try to keep us from getting photographs of their vehicle. We may have to go to a judge, and a litigation setting, to get those photographs, but if our client has taken photographs of the scene, giving us a perspective of their own vehicle and the other vehicle, that is extremely helpful. That's probably the single most important thing to do at the scene.

Obtain contact information: Try to get names and contact information from witnesses. Most of the time the police will put this information in their report, but sometimes they miss witnesses who might leave the scene shortly after the accident.

In the immediate aftermath

You have a duty to file a claim—that is, call in and report the accident—to your insurance company. When you call it in, you get a claim number. Make sure you write down the claim number and keep it handy, because all your medical care, until the PIP is exhausted, will be processed through that claim number.

When you go see a doctor, you give them your claim number, and they will process your care through the claim number. To be eligible for PIP benefits, you have to see a doctor within 14 days after the accident, and a medical doctor has to determine that you have an emergency medical condition, or the $10,000 PIP benefit is reduced to $2,500.

PIP also covers lost wages, but that all comes out of the same pot of money, so you should let your lawyer know right away if you are unable to work. You will need a note from the doctor verifying that you can't work, and then you can ask your lawyer to send a letter to the insurance company, reserving money for lost wages. Otherwise, they will just pay out all the money to the emergency room or the doctors and if you're out of work for a month or two, you won't get that lost wage money, because it's all gone to the doctors. The lawyer can try to reserve some of that money for you.

There's a standard form that insurance companies use when there's a lost wage claim. It's easiest if there's an employer and the employer fills out the form showing your wages. The insurance companies use that form to average your last 13 weeks' wages and then they pay you 60 percent of that average. It's more problematic when a person is self-employed. You typically have to show your tax records for the year and average it out for the month. They'll calculate what a week is worth, and pay you 60 percent for each week that you're out of work until the PIP is exhausted.

When the $10,000 PIP is used up, you will need to turn to your own health insurance. Although the wrongdoer's insurance company is liable for your medical bills, they don't start out paying your medical bills. They don't pay your physical therapy bills. They don't pay your lost wages. They don't pay anything, in fact. People typically think that if it's the other guy's fault, they'll pay for ongoing medical treatment, but that's not the way it happens.

What you need is an <u>Exhaustion of Benefits</u> letter from your insurance company, which verifies that all your benefits are used up. Then you have your physician contact your health insurance provider—Blue Cross, Aetna, Medicare, whatever it is—and they will bill that provider.

The wrongdoer's insurance company will <u>not</u> pay as you go. What happens is that at the conclusion of the case, your lawyer will negotiate one lump sum settlement. That settlement will take care of the medical bills that you've already incurred, your future medical bills, your past lost wages, and your future loss of earning capacity, as well as your pain and suffering if there is a permanent injury.

Duty to Cooperate: Paperwork

Your own insurance company will want you to give a taped phone statement about the accident. If you've already seen a lawyer, typically your lawyer will sit in on that statement. That's one reason why you should get a lawyer fairly quickly.

On the other hand, we often get the case after the client has already given a statement to the insurance company. One purpose of the insurance company taking this statement is to look for facts upon which they can deny coverage. For instance, if the driver of your car was a relative who lives with you, but you didn't report when you took out the policy that this person was living with you, they will deny coverage, saying that you're guilty of a material misrepresentation. That's why having an attorney is a good idea.

The lawyer will help you deal with your own insurance company as well as the other party's insurance company. You owe a duty to your insurance company, to cooperate with them, but at the same time, your insurance company has the right—and they do this frequently—to try and cut off your benefits. In addition to taking a statement from you, they will send you paperwork that you have to sign, which gives them access to your medical records. You will have to describe in detail how the accident happened and what your injuries are.

We usually just do that paperwork as a courtesy for our clients. It's an <u>application for benefits</u>; we get the application filled out and submitted. Your doctor also has to send paperwork to your insurance company; it's called an <u>attending physician's statement,</u> and will usually be sent to you to give to your doctor by your insurance company.

Dealing with property damage

Property damage is a part of any auto accident case. As I described in Chapter 9, if the accident is not your fault, the other party's insurance should cover your property damage. If you have collision coverage on your own insurance, you may opt to go through your own policy. Though you will have to pay a deductible, your own insurance may be quicker, and your company will eventually recover that deductible for you from the other party.

If you go through the other party's company, it's usually slower because they're not going to accept liability right away. They are going to wait until they get a copy of the accident report and talk to the insured and make sure that it's their fault. Only then will they accept liability. They will often provide compensation for a rental car while your car is in the shop being repaired or they will compensate you for a rental until they make the decision to cut you a check.

Of course in order to rent a vehicle, you need a credit card, and some people don't have credit cards. They can't rent a vehicle. But if you have a credit card, you can rent a vehicle, and most of the time, we can get full compensation for the rental vehicle from the defendant's insurance company.

An alternative is to wait until they accept liability, and then they will frequently do a direct billing. They'll give you the defendant's claim number and tell you to go to Enterprise or whichever rental company they use, and the rental company will bill the insurance directly. Sometimes you have to pay a dollar or two extra for insurance, but that's generally the way it works.

The biggest problem with property damage comes when you owe more on the car than the value of the car. They will pay to fix the car, typically, unless the damage is more than 80 percent of the car's value. When it's a total loss, you are sort of stuck with the value that the insurance company sets, and if you purchased a car that has depreciated greatly and you owe more on it, it could be a real problem. Depending on your circumstances, you may want to add gap insurance to your auto policy to avoid this situation. Gap insurance covers the difference between the car's actual value and the financing, so that you don't owe money on a car that has been destroyed.

What I usually tell clients is we're going to get money back at the end of the case out of the personal injury aspect, and hopefully we'll get a little extra to compensate them for any loss they take on a property damage issue.

As the case unfolds

Your lawyer will talk with you about evaluating your case (as in Chapter 5), taking into account your injuries, the liability, and all of the insurance coverages. There is a whole range of factors to consider in these kinds of cases.

Figuring out the coverages is important. The nature of the impact is important. If there's a big impact, the case usually has more value, but what's tricky is that there is not necessarily a one-on-one relationship between impact and injury. Think of a football player on the field. There can be a big hit, and the player just gets up and runs back to the huddle. Or he could be hit at the wrong angle and end with a significant injury.

Auto accidents are a bit like that, but insurance companies typically don't want to pay in a low-impact situation. So low-impact accidents present their own challenges, and there are various other factors that we have to look at.

Low impact

For example, I have one case where my client was a car salesman on a test drive with a customer, and at the time of the impact he was turned towards the driver of the car. He was in the passenger seat at the time of the accident, and he was at a fairly acute angle. Because he was sitting at such an acute angle, he was not as cushioned by the seat back, so there was a higher propensity for an injury, even though it was a relatively low impact.

The objective evidence of injury is important, but it is not something that we can size up immediately, unless the client has been hospitalized, with fractures or some sort of significant injuries, or we have photographs that show black eyes or cuts and bruises.

Very frequently, the objective nature of the injury is documented through radiographic tests ordered by the treating physician down the road. The average x-ray or CT scan in the emergency room is really done to rule out some sort of acute injury; it doesn't generally reveal a more subtle injury.

There is a whole range of tests that can be used to diagnose these more subtle injuries, such as nerve conduction tests. The gold standard is the MRI, for instance, to show a disc injury, which can be quite serious.

Insurance companies frequently try to dispute the results of radiographic tests. If the case is litigated, or sometimes even if it is not, they will obtain the original images to have them read by their own experts. The problem with that is that their experts aren't necessarily objective.

There's no rhyme or reason to this, but in a certain percentage of cases, insurance companies will try to cut off your benefits. It usually happens several months after the crash if they think that you're over-treating with a physical therapist or a chiropractor.

Compulsory Medical Evaluation

The company may send you to their doctor for what's called a compulsory medical examination (CME). This can happen through your own company if you are claiming PIP benefits, or through the other party's insurance company if there is litigation.

The doctors hired to conduct these CMEs usually contend that a whiplash or soft tissue injury will always be better in a few weeks, but that's just not the case. These kinds of injuries can last for a long time. They're difficult to diagnose and treat because the damage—say a stretched or torn ligament—is deep inside your body and doesn't show up on a traditional x-ray. For these doctors to suggest that everyone is always going to get better from a whiplash injury in four weeks seems to me really unfair. It's not acting in good faith.

When there is a CME ordered, we talk to our clients about it. Sometimes we get a protective order. We frequently send a videographer to accompany the client. Often these doctors will do a detailed history and then do just a two-minute physical examination. We want to catch that on video because we can use it if we have to cross-examine the doctor at deposition or trial.

During treatment

In a typical auto accident, you would have a choice between different kinds of medical providers, generally either a medical doctor or a chiropractor. If the client doesn't have a provider, the lawyer can provide suggestions of providers who handle these kinds of cases. A lot of primary care physicians really don't want to deal with these kinds of cases. They don't want to get involved in the legal system so you have to go out of your way to find someone who can deal with these kinds of cases. It's not so much the specialty as it is the doctor's willingness to deal with these cases and their experience in treating accident cases. There are neurologists, orthopedists, rehabilitation doctors, osteopathic doctors, and even family doctors who have accident and injury clinics. It's a matter of knowing which doctors in your community are willing not only to treat the patient but also to provide the necessary written report on the injuries and treatment. The lawyer can help with that.

The lawyer maintains contact with the client throughout his or her treatment, and should be telling the client we're here for you. Remember that because it's a contingency contract, contact with the lawyer or the lawyer's staff does not result in additional fees. From my point of view, I get to know the client better if I have some additional contact so I want the client to talk to me about the course of their treatment. Of course, I'm a lawyer, not a doctor. I don't try to practice medicine, but I've had plenty of experience in dealing with both accident victims and doctors, so I can put my two cents in. I always advise the client to listen to their doctor, but I may suggest they ask their doctor to send them to this or that specialist. In our area, there are specific orthopedists who deal with spinal injuries, or hand injuries, or shoulder injuries. So hiring a lawyer who is familiar with the medical personnel in their community can pay dividends for the client who is the patient and is trying to recover from these injuries.

Reducing stress, guiding the client

The lawyer is trying to do two or three things at once, to help take the stress of this situation off the client. The average client can be overwhelmed in dealing with the aftermath of an accident because it's not intuitive and the insurance companies are not necessarily out to help you. So it's important to have a lawyer help you through it. There's a lot of stress: not just the physical injury, but the psychological stress of maybe not being able to work, with a resultant loss of income, and the stress of dealing with insurance companies. The companies' goals are not your goals; they're just trying to do what they can to get the claim resolved with minimal expense to the insurance company. They are not necessarily trying to help the client.

So the lawyer needs to interpose himself between the client and the insurance company with the goal of reducing all this stress. Let your lawyer take the stress of dealing with this. The more stress you have, the worse you're going to feel. Your muscles are going to tighten up, and that doesn't help your physical recovery.

What we do is try to take away the psychological stress, help the client deal with the insurance company in an unusual situation, offering them some guidance about the medical treatment while encouraging them to follow their doctor's advice. At the same time we counsel them about the expectations of where the case is going and try to get the best case results for them. Occasionally, if we think it appropriate, we will immediately advise them to file a lawsuit. More often, we will wait for the client to get to maximum medical improvement (MMI), as indicated by the doctor's report. At that point we put together the demand package, as described in Chapter 4. We send it to the insurance company requesting a response within 30 days.

When the insurance company responds, we communicate that to the client, and tell them what we think the client should do. We may advise them to settle the case, but usually we recommend rejecting the first offer and negotiating a bit. If we feel that a reasonable settlement is unlikely, we advise filing a lawsuit, but the client always makes the final decision. The lawyer is there to act on the client's decisions but try and guide the client in the best way possible.

Points to Remember

1. Call law enforcement.

2. Obtain medical attention.

3. Preserve evidence through photos.

4. Hire competent attorney.

5. Follow through.

*For a more detailed check list please see 7 Mistakes to Avoid on page 169.

Chapter 11: Tractor Trailer Accidents

AS YOU MIGHT EXPECT there are many similarities between auto accidents and tractor trailer accidents, but there are some key differences to note. For one thing, the stakes are generally much higher: Injuries are often severe and insurance limits are usually higher. There are usually multiple parties involved. For instance, you have to be aware that a trailer can be leased; there could be a negligent hiring claim, regarding an "independent contractor" who may actually be an employee of a different corporation with higher insurance limits.

Dealing with tractor trailer accidents requires some particular expertise because there is a whole separate set of rules and regulations that apply to tractor trailers. There are different rules for interstate and intrastate trucks, and you have to know the difference. Commercial trucking and tractor trailers are governed by a set of rules called the Federal Motor Carrier Safety Regulations (FMCSR). These are rules promulgated by the federal Department of Transportation, and they cover a lot of things regarding truck drivers and trucking companies.

Fatigue

For instance, there are very strict rules regarding driver fatigue, placing limits on the number of consecutive hours a driver can drive and how many hours they can drive in a week. Drivers are required to keep logs documenting their driving time, and as a plaintiff's lawyer we frequently have to obtain these records.

Trucking experts

These cases tend to rely heavily on experts. With a major truck accident we usually want to get an accident reconstruction engineer out to the scene as soon as possible. We may also hire truck driving experts, people who can talk about what the drivers did or did not do wrong.

In additionally, it may be necessary to hire experts in the FMCSR so we can talk about which regulations apply, which regulations were violated, how they were violated, and why they were violated in this particular case. Because there is so much more at stake—more severe injuries and much higher insurance limits—the defense will fight hard on these cases. They will hire the best experts their money can buy, they will try to hire good lawyers, and you're in for a fight when you have one of these cases. The plaintiff's attorneys have to be willing to spend the money to hire the right experts in these situations because the defendants will always try to do their utmost to defeat your claim.

On the other hand, juries are often more receptive to cases where a trucking company or truck driver violates the law, resulting in someone being hurt or maimed or even killed. These cases frequently get valued more fairly than regular auto accidents.

Case Study: Log truck negligence

As I'm writing this book, we have been litigating and settling a significant trucking case. My client—let's call him

Mr. Ford—was driving home from work at night, on a 65 mile-an-hour road. He's worked for this same employer for 30 years, so he has driven this road thousands of times. This one time, there was a tractor trailer that had pulled across the roadway and was blocking both lanes. Mr. Ford saw the truck; he left 75 feet of skid marks before he ran into it. The defense is arguing that—despite their driver pulling across the roadway at night and blocking the roadway—our client was comparatively negligent for not seeing the truck earlier.

I should explain what I mean by comparatively negligent. The defense in this case is claiming that our client was partly responsible for the accident. Every state has its own laws concerning negligence, or fault. Florida is a comparative negligence state. That means that if a defendant pleads that the plaintiff was comparatively negligent, a jury would have to determine what percent of the fault to attribute to the defendant and what percent to attribute to the plaintiff. It has to add up to 100 percent. Suppose the damages are $100,000 and the jury decides that the plaintiff is 40 percent liable and the defendant is 60 percent liable, then the judge would enter a judgment for $60,000 against the defendant.

In our case, the basic argument is over conspicuity, which is a fancy legal term for visibility. The FMCSR requires trucks to have certain numbers of lights, reflectors, and reflective tape in order to meet visibility standards. Before these standards were established, there were studies showing that a lot of accidents involving trucks happened because the trucks weren't visible enough on the highway.

We hear lots of talk these days about too much regulation, but the truth is that a lot of federal regulations are common sense. They save lives, they save money, and they're necessary. The federal government commissioned studies to determine the best ways to provide visibility for large commercial trucks, and established regulations according to what the studies found. So now, in addition to the required lights, there is a retroreflective tape to be applied to the trucks. It's simple. The tape needs to be red and white in an even pattern that's easy for an individual to recognize, and it needs to outline the corners of the vehicle, so other drivers can appreciate the size and shape of the truck. The tape has to be half the distance of the trailer that the truck is towing, and it should be put as close to the ends as possible so the trailer is outlined, and it can be seen from a significant distance away.

In our case, the tractor trailer was not taped properly. The defense is trying to blame our client for a visibility issue when the truck driver and the trucking company were not complying with the visibility regulations in the FMCSR. Of course, this means that we now have experts about the federal rules as they relate to this tape.

In this case each side has hired a truck driving expert, who deals with expectations, training, and the art of truck driving and an accident reconstruction expert, who is basically an engineer dealing with issues of time, speed, and difference. The defense also went and hired a conspicuity expert to testify about the visibility of the tape on the side of the truck. Their expert never saw the vehicle or tested the vehicle. He's working from a book that says in this circumstance and with this tape job, the truck should have been seen from this distance. We filed a motion with the court to strike the defense expert under a famous federal case called Daubert and the judge granted our motion. Thus we knocked out a key defense witness.

The defense also hired another expert. This expert testified that in his interpretation of the FMCSR, the driver didn't have to make sure that the tape was adequate. The responsibility was only applicable to the manufacturers. My daughter is working with me on this case, and she's very good at the discovery process. Julie wants to leave no stone unturned.

She was able to obtain the state registration for the trailer. The trailer was built in 1990. There's a specific FMCSR which says that for all trailers built prior to 1992, it is the driver's responsibility to make sure that they are retrofitted in conformity with the current regulation. The defense testimony was totally neutralized by our detailed approach.

All cases are different but these are examples of how, in trucking cases, you have to understand what the issues are, get the right experts, and pursue the cases vigorously because the other side doesn't want to pay. If you are involved in a case like this, you need an attorney who's willing to litigate, go to bat for you, hire the right experts, and pursue the case in order to get the best result. The insurance company for the log truck driver has recently tendered their full policy limits.

Points to Remember

1. Look for FMCSR violations.

2. Look for multiple defendants.

3. Hire experts in truck driving practices, federal regulations, and accident reconstruction.

4. Download electronic data if available.

Chapter 12: Wrongful Death

AS WE'VE BEEN DISCUSSING, the essence of personal injury law is dealing with cases in which one person has been injured through someone else's negligence. Sometimes the injury is so severe that it causes a death. A <u>wrongful death case</u> is a particular type of negligence case where someone has been killed. The case is brought on behalf of the survivors of the deceased person.

Wrongful death cases can stem from many situations: automobile accidents, plane or train crashes, medical malpractice, day care or nursing home negligence, workplace accidents, defective products, and dangerous property conditions are some examples.

Dealing with a wrongful death case is always difficult from a psychological point of view, because the tragedy is so enormous: A family has been deprived of a loved one. There's nothing the lawyer can do about that but encourage them to cherish the memories and help them find some recourse in the legal process.

When people come to us after a wrongful death, I have found they are rarely motivated by financial considerations. Sometimes they are extremely upset; sometimes they're analytical about it; sometimes they're simply looking for justice.

Often they are looking for something—anything—that they can do to keep this horrible situation from happening to other families. For example, if it's a drunk driving situation, or some kind of product liability, they'll ask how they can make things better in the future, or what they can do to stop this kind of behavior. Unfortunately, I have to tell them that the legal system is not set up to stop bad behavior; all we can do is seek compensation after the behavior has already happened.

In many ways these cases proceed as other personal injury cases, but there are some specific statutes that apply to wrongful death cases. For example, the statute of limitations is shorter. The average negligence case has a four-year statute of limitations; for wrongful death it's only two years. A claim for wrongful death can only be brought by the personal representative of the deceased's estate, so navigating these cases requires some expertise in probate law and estate law, and sometimes guardianship law as well.

The Florida Wrongful Death Law sets forth specific categories of damages, defines who can make a claim, and describes how an individual can make a claim. So when a family comes in, we explain the steps necessary to pursue a wrongful death case. My wife Cherie and I often meet jointly with these families because Cherie does the probate work. Probate refers to the process under which a judge oversees the transfer of assets according to a will if the person had one, or determines what happens with various items if a person dies intestate, meaning without a will. After any death assets have to be transferred—like personal property, or real estate, or the title to a car—and so a wrongful death case is also subject to the probate process.

When we meet with a family, we not only ascertain the facts of the case, but we also inform them that an estate has to be opened, and a personal representative has to be appointed. If there are minor children, a guardian frequently has to be appointed. If the survivors are adult children, then one of them has to be designated as the personal representative of the estate. He or she is acting for the benefit of all the others, and the estate is distributed equally or at least pursuant to the law in the wrongful death statute.

What exactly is a <u>personal representative</u>? The personal representative—sometimes called an <u>executor</u>—is the person in charge of the estate after a death. That person is frequently named in a will, but when there is no will, we have to apply to the court for a personal representative appointment. It is the decision of the personal representative to hire a particular law firm to pursue a wrongful death case.

In any event, even if there are no personal items of property or real estate, in order to maintain a wrongful death case, an estate needs to be opened in the probate process. By opening an estate we mean that paperwork needs to be filed, and at the courthouse, a file is opened by the clerk of court under the supervision of a judge, entitled "The Estate of X," where X is the name of the deceased individual. The estate is opened by the personal representative, and that must be done before a wrongful death claim can be made.

Sometimes there are competing claims: if a child is deceased and the parents are either divorced or not on the same page, there can be a fight about who will be the personal representative. Florida law does specify who has priority to be appointed as the personal representative. If there are competing claims, it can come down to the decision of a judge.

For instance, in the event of a death of an unmarried individual with minor children, the children's guardian or parent would have a preference over another family member. These priorities make sense, but there is some discretion with the judge in reaching these decisions.

It's part of our representation, when we open a wrongful death file, to do the probate ourselves. We keep it in house, meaning it's the same law firm. Other law firms will farm it out to a law firm that does nothing but probate work. We do our own probate work because we feel that we can do a good job, and we get to know the families better that way. We've had good success on contested cases regarding who is appointed the personal representative.

Once the personal representative is appointed by the court, it is the personal representative's decision whether or not to bring a lawsuit for wrongful death. Usually the personal representative will have retained us and we would give the personal representative advice on whether they have a case, whether a lawsuit should be brought, and against whom the lawsuit should be brought.

Usually when an individual dies, and he or she is survived by parents or children, a claim can be brought by either the parents or the children, just depending on the ages and the situation. There are a few exceptions, though. For instance, the lobby representing physicians persuaded the Florida legislature to pass a law saying that when medical negligence kills an individual, but that individual is not survived by minor children, their adult children cannot make a claim for medical malpractice. Parents of an adult child can't make a claim for medical malpractice, no matter how damaged they have been. They may have had a great relationship with their adult child, and be deeply damaged by the loss, but they cannot make a claim. So sometimes we have the unfortunate duty of telling people who call us, "Well, I'm sorry, but we can't pursue a wrongful death claim for you."

Once a wrongful death case has been filed and is being pursued, there are a number of other considerations that come into play. In dealing with the loss of a loved one, there may be emotional and psychological damages to the survivors, so once again we're back into the realm of the expert witness. The attorney meets with the family, evaluating the horrible loss and determining whether some sort of grief expert or psychologist or counselor needs to be retained as an expert witness. Similarly, we might retain an expert witness for purposes of evaluating the lost support—not just the salary, but everything that the deceased individual did for the family—in an effort to try and quantify some of those losses.

Naturally, as in any case, we have to prove fault on the part of the defendant. We may need to hire an accident reconstruction expert or other engineer, as we would in an auto accident case. In these cases the stakes can be much higher for the family deprived of a loved one and/or a breadwinner; the damages can be so enormous under those circumstances.

Once the attorney makes a recovery in a wrongful death case, we may need to look further and try to determine the best disposition of the assets for the individual. If it's a minor child who's very young, we will already have had a guardian appointed. But then we need to go back to the court, assuming we've made the recovery, and propose a plan for the disposition of the assets.

Minor children

In the state of Florida, when young children are left without a parent, then the guardian has the ability to spend some of the estate assets to support and help the children in a way determined by the trial court. So it's the responsibility of the attorney in that situation just to make sure that the estate funds that he has helped generate for the children's benefit are utilized in a way that best enhances their continued development living without their dad or their mom. That's a big responsibility and we take it extremely seriously. We don't want to just make a recovery in the case; we want to try to provide for the development and the best interests of the children as they grow up.

Case Study: Wrongful death

We recently settled a complex wrongful death case involving minors. A father of two young children was killed in an auto accident; he was a passenger in the vehicle. It's a good example of how many factors can serve to complicate cases like this.

In this case, the young man who was killed was not married to the mother of his children, so there was some dispute over who would be the personal representative. We wound up hiring a prominent local attorney to serve as the personal representative; the mother was eventually appointed guardian to the children.

To make things even more difficult, the accident happened in another state, so we were dealing with not only Florida law but the laws of the other state as well. Even though the insurance company had agreed to settle with the estate, and we'd received approval from the probate judge in Florida, the company insisted that we go to the state where the accident occurred. It happened to be the policy in that state that the money would be kept in trust until the children were 18. That meant that no money would be available for the raising of the children, despite the fact that the father had been the family breadwinner.

In the meantime, the defendant in the case declared bankruptcy and got a bankruptcy judge to absolve him of all debt. So we had to get an order from the bankruptcy judge saying we could go ahead with our case to the extent of the insurance, which had already been agreed to.

This is how complicated it got: We ended up hiring seven different lawyers: a guardianship lawyer; a probate lawyer, who was Cherie; a lawyer as personal representative; a lawyer to help with the out-of-state bankruptcy up there; an attorney ad litem here to report to the probate judge; an attorney ad litem up there to report to the judge from whom we were seeking approval, and a personal injury lawyer in the other state. We then flew up there to present the matter to the out-of-state judge, and fortunately, were able to persuade him that the money should be released to the probate court in Florida.

We felt very strongly that we needed to get the money released back to Florida so a court could determine, after being presented with a financial plan, the best solution for the children. We wanted the funds to be able to substitute for their dad's income as they grew; the children were very young when their dad died.

Eventually we ended up making a substantial recovery for the two children. And we set up meetings for their mother with a financial advisor so that the money obtained in the recovery can be invested and utilized in the best way possible for those children. Should some of the money be preserved for them for when they reached 18? Absolutely. But the most important thing is that money be available for their mom to utilize in bringing them up. If they need braces, if they need medical care, if she needs transportation, if she needs housing or food—all those things need to be provided for. Hopefully, as a result of our efforts, those needs will be met in this particular situation.

Another wrongful death case goes back some years, but it was particularly significant for me personally because it gave me the opportunity to argue an appeal in front of the Supreme Court of Florida.

Case Study: Employer liability for wrongful death

The case involved an explosion at a chemical plant that killed one technician and seriously injured another, leaving him with permanent brain damage. The company contended that it was simply a workers' compensation case; we argued that the company was liable under an exception for wrongful acts that which were "substantially certain" to injure an individual. The law had been on the books in Florida for years, but no employee had ever been able to use it to sue an employer.

The company in question was developing a process to make some particular chemical compounds, and they were utilizing some chemicals that were incredibly volatile. These were things that could explode on contact with oxygen, or if they were compressed, or even if they were shaken hard.

As they were experimenting and developing this process on a small scale, they had a series of explosions in the plant, so they established a series of safety precautions. These said, for instance, that if you're going to mix these chemicals to try and make this substance, we'll do it by remote control. The worker would go behind a barrier and press a button, and by remote control the chemicals would be mixed together.

Then the company was approached by a large corporation that offered them a huge amount of money to produce large quantities of this compound. So they were trying to scale up their process—to make gallons and gallons at a time instead of just a pint or so—and in doing so, they disregarded some of the safety protocols that had been in place for the past 18 months.

When our clients were hurt, they had been directed by their supervisors to mix large quantities of these chemicals and shake them manually. As experienced technicians they might have been hesitant, but they were ordered by their supervisors to shake it manually, despite the fact that in the past it had been done in small quantities, remotely, behind barriers.

As you might expect, there was an explosion. One of the clients was killed, and another client was brain damaged, and we took the case.

The issue in the case was the fact that they were employees, and never before in Florida legal history had employees been able to sue their employer. The proposed remedy by the insurance company was just to take the workers' comp benefits, which are very limited. There was supposedly an exclusion for tortious acts, or wrongful acts, which were substantially certain to injure an individual, but no court had ever found that the acts of an employee rose to that level.

We argued the case in front of a local circuit judge, and we were unsuccessful. The circuit judge granted the defense motion for summary judgment. But because we believed so much in the case, we took it to the First District Court of Appeal to try to overturn the summary judgment. Unfortunately we lost again, but the appellate court conceded that there might be something to our position, and suggested that the Supreme Court of Florida take a look at the issue. So that gave us another chance.

We appealed it to the Supreme Court of Florida, and I got to argue the matter in front of the Supreme Court. It's a big deal in the life of any lawyer when he gets to do an appellate argument, and particularly when he gets to do an appellate argument in the court of highest jurisdiction in your state. We drove up to Tallahassee, and I brought my whole family to watch: my mother, my son, my daughter, my wife, and my partner. The seven justices came into the courtroom, and we started.

The argument went fairly well, and the end result of the case was that for the first time in Florida history, the Supreme Court of Florida decided that an individual could sue his employer under the substantial certainty test that had been listed in the Florida statutes for decades, but had never been tested. It was a unanimous decision; all seven justices ruled for us. I was extremely pleased with being able to argue the case and argue it successfully.

Temporary Hero

For about six months to a year, I was a hero among plaintiffs' lawyers. I was asked to speak at various seminars. People would call and ask me how I did it, because the opinions are published statewide, and all the lawyers saw that this was a great change in the law. They thought it was wonderful. My clients thought it was wonderful because we were able to settle the case. The defendants did not want to risk taking the case to trial, so they voluntarily paid the substantial settlement.

Unfortunately, there were several groups that really didn't like the result in that case, and one group was the Florida legislature. From a political point of view, the Florida legislature was not enlightened or supportive when it came to damages for victims. They only were concerned with the fact that workers' compensation insurance rates might go up. Lobbyists for the insurance industry got busy persuading legislators to make some changes to the law. So, about a year after the Supreme Court ruled our way, the legislature passed a law making it far more difficult to bring this kind of case. They changed "substantial certainty" to "virtual certainty," and they changed the legal standard of proof.

This case and the legislative response to the opinion of the Supreme Court of Florida illustrate how lobbyists for business interests prioritize profits over people.

Points to Remember

1. Estate must be opened.

2. A personal representative must be appointed.

3. Guardianships for minor children are sometimes required.

4. Experts can include psychologists, economists, and accident reconstruction engineers.

5. Florida law is very specific as to who can claim damages.

Chapter 13: Premises Liability
—Slip and Fall

"SLIP AND FALL" is a type of premises liability case. A premises liability case is a personal injury case in which someone is injured as a result of an unsafe condition on someone else's property.

Slip-and-falls are, to a certain extent, different from auto cases, partly because there is often a negative public perception of these cases. But the injuries in cases like this can be significant. In these kinds of cases we often do see fractures and surgeries, whether it's someone landing on a shoulder or someone breaking a leg or breaking a foot. Our firm typically doesn't take a slip-and-fall case unless the injury is significant, because we know that the insurance companies defend these cases vigorously, so there's probably a higher percentage that we have to litigate.

When someone calls me about a potential slip-and-fall case, I focus on two things: the liability and the injury. Regarding the liability, I usually want to see photographs of the area. If the injured victim has photographs that they've taken with their cell phone, I ask them to email those to me. I'll show them to the other lawyers to get their opinion.

Suppose, for example, it's a sidewalk issue. The sidewalk isn't level—maybe a portion of the slab is sticking up, or maybe there's a hole in the walkway—so it causes a fall and injury. Here's a tip: When you take a photograph of that sidewalk, take a ruler with you and include it in the photo, to document the amount of the deviation from the level surface. The photograph isn't enough; it needs the sense of perspective that comes from having a ruler or other measuring tool in it. Then we can make a more informed decision on the potential case.

Insurance limits are frequently higher in these cases because we're often dealing with businesses. Sometimes we're dealing with municipalities—sovereign local cities or counties—so we may also be dealing with some immunity issues.

Because of all these factors, we screen slip-and-fall cases a little differently than we do the typical auto accident. We want to see the photos and we want to know about the significance of the injuries. If the potential client says, "My back is hurting or my leg is hurting," we'll ask them to see a doctor first and then come back to us. It doesn't make sense—for us or for the client—to open a file in these cases unless the injury is serious. Having said that, we have made recoveries in the hundreds of thousands of dollars when there is a serious injury and liability is clear.

Let me offer a couple of examples. In one case, our client was at a car dealership. The dealership had a gutter coming off the roof and discharging into the parking lot. When the client fell in the parking lot and was injured, the EMTs who responded to the incident noted that the parking lot was really slippery in that location and they have trouble staying upright. There was green slime, the algae that can develop, at least in the state of Florida, when an area is kept consistently wet. As in any personal injury case, it's important to get all the records, including the EMT records, but when you have a record like that, it really helps the liability claim. In this case, where the individual was seriously injured, we were able to make a nice recovery.

In another case, our client was working at an old house that was being renovated. She was measuring for blinds when suddenly the floor gave out beneath her and she fell through the floor. Her injuries were significant. We did have to litigate, but we were able to make a good recovery for her. On one of my earliest cases, our client was invited to walk in an attic to do some surveying for a construction issue. He fell right through the attic flooring because it was inadequate, and he suffered a serious heel fracture. We had to litigate, but we made a recovery there also.

Contrary to what many people believe when they hear about slip-and-falls, the cases that attorneys litigate and make recoveries in are typically very serious injuries. The reason people get hurt in these incidents is that they are usually trying to react to something unforeseen that has happened.

In a typical supermarket or store case, the issue might be a substance left on the floor. In that event, you do need to show that it wasn't just left in the last 30 seconds because then the store might not be liable. But if the substance had some shoe tracks in it indicating it had been on the floor for a while, that could enhance a liability argument.

Points to Remember

1. Must show negligence.
2. Negligence can be in design or operation.
3. Preserve evidence with photos of dangerous condition.
4. Look for video evidence.

Chapter 14: Premises Liability— Negligent Security for Criminal Attacks

ONE OF MY FIRST FORAYS into personal injury law was actually a premises liability case. The clients were a married couple who had come to Gainesville for medical treatment, and they were attacked in their apartment. The husband was disabled and they were sexually assaulted by an individual. A deputy sheriff gave them my name as someone who might be able to help them pursue a case.

I did a search of prior police records for the apartment complex to look for criminal activity. The complex was an L-shaped series of small apartment buildings, four apartments to each building. One leg of the "L" bordered on woods, and my clients' apartment was in the middle of that section. There was no fence and there was bad lighting. Somewhat predictably, the records showed that the building adjacent to the woods, where there was no fence and no good lighting, had been burglarized eight times in the past four years. That established a necessary predicate to making the premises liability case. Then I hired an expert to testify that a criminal action was foreseeable and the owners of the apartment building were negligent because they didn't provide good lighting or good fencing and they did nothing to alleviate the conditions that allowed the attack. No security guards were ever hired by the landlord despite the repetitive series of burglaries.

Case Study: Danny Rolling

That case led to my being involved in a couple of other premises liability cases where there were attacks by a third party. The most serious cases involved serial killer Danny Rolling. In 1990, Mr. Rolling went on a burglary and murder spree. He attacked and murdered students from the University of Florida, after breaking into their apartments. He lived in the woods—these were crimes of opportunity—and he would be looking at an apartment where there were girls that attracted him. He was attracted to a particular physical type, and he would then break into the apartment. Mr. Rolling was eventually caught. He was arrested, prosecuted by the local state attorney, convicted and eventually sentenced to death.

But when the murders happened, the town was in a panic. There was a series of these murders, five in all, over a few weeks. The murders were unsolved. People were just walking around town, looking nervously around them, not knowing who would be the next target. The attacks were all within a certain part of town where there were a lot of student apartments and I ended up representing two of the families.

Once the first family retained my office, I immediately went to the apartment. I saw that the sliding door had been put on backwards. The apartment building had no security, no good lighting, and no good fencing. To a disturbed criminal like Danny Rolling, it was obviously an invitation to an attack.

After a Miami law firm turned down a second victimized family I was retained to investigate liability for that attack.

We were successful in both cases. We did file lawsuits, but we settled the cases. I was very careful to keep the cases low key; I didn't want to give Danny Rolling any sort of public venue while the criminal case was going on.

In the first case, in addition to suing the apartment complex, we sued the manufacturer of the sliding glass door. Danny Rolling often popped sliding glass doors off their tracks to gain entrance to the apartments. This company manufactured a door which seemed to be incapable of being secured. When a door slides to the inside, you can put a broom handle in the track and it makes it very difficult to get in. This door, however, was designed so it slid to the outside. So in addition to suing the apartment complex, we made a product liability claim against the manufacturer of the door. The company went into bankruptcy shortly before our claim, but eventually the claim was preserved and we were able to make a recovery when they emerged from bankruptcy.

Back then, we established a practice, whenever we would successfully resolve a wrongful death case, of trying to contribute something back to society and help grieving families take some meaning from their sudden loss. With one of the cases that we resolved, the murder victim was a student at Santa Fe Community College and we endowed a scholarship at Santa Fe Community College in the name of the victim. It's a perpetual scholarship, so there are still students receiving these scholarships today. On behalf of another victim, we donated to a foundation in her hometown.

Murderers should not profit from their crimes

Perhaps the most important public service we performed as a result of these tragic criminal attacks took place after the personal injury cases had resolved. We became aware that Danny Rolling through his "girlfriend" was preparing to publish a book which was a thinly fictionalized account of his horrific murders. We filed a lawsuit on behalf of the families pursuant to a Florida law which restricted murderers from profiting as a result of their criminal activity. The lawsuit was joined by our competent and ethical State Attorney, Rod Smith, who eventually obtained an injection prohibiting publication. I was pleased to have spearheaded the initiation of this successful lawsuit.

From these few examples, you can see that premises liability cases can vary widely, including everything from simple slip-and-fall incidents to criminal attacks by third parties. They can include a whole variety of theories, but I did develop an expertise in the area of premises liability after handling a number of these cases, and continue to pursue these matters when innocent victims are seriously injured through the fault of another.

Points to Remember

1. Attack must be foreseeable.

2. Obtain police records of crime at that location

3. Utilize expert(s) to show deficiencies in lighting, fencing, locks, and/or security patrols.

Chapter 15: Bicycle Accidents

I HAVE A DEEP AFFINITY for cyclists. It is human nature. I sometimes ride my bike to work, I support the Gainesville Cycling Club, and many of our family vacations have been through bicycle tour companies. I am deeply concerned when I see serious injuries to cyclists.

Unlike automobile accidents, the issue of "low impact" does not arise in these cases. We frequently see multiple fractures and other serious injuries. It is important to be familiar with the Florida Statutes and laws in Chapter 316 of the statutes. Cyclists can be considered pedestrians when on sidewalks, but also have to comply with the laws governing the traffic control devices and rules. There is some degree of animosity against cyclists by drivers, which is very unfortunate.

As noted in the checklist above, cyclists are covered under their own PIP if struck by another motor vehicle. Likewise, they are covered under other insurance policy provisions, including UM. As in auto cases generally, the health insurance would be a valid backup once the initial coverage is exhausted.

Motorist negligence is the predominant cause of cycling injuries. I rarely see situations where the cyclist is negligent, but the necessity to ride defensively is critical in these unfortunate cases. I have been able to recover million dollar settlements without filing a lawsuit in some of my cycling cases, but I still believe an aggressive approach is best.

Points to Remember

1. May be covered by your own auto PIP for medical bills.

2. Can be covered by defendant's PIP if you or family member do not own car.

3. As in auto accidents, take photos, get medical attention, call law enforcement.

4. Property damage is covered by at-fault defendant's auto insurance.

5. Look for video and/or black box download.

Chapter 16: Specific Types of Injuries

IN AN EARLIER CHAPTER, I mentioned that your personal injury lawyer should keep in touch with you throughout the course of medical treatment for your injury. A lawyer who handles personal injury cases does develop at least a little bit of knowledge of anatomy, medical nomenclature, and how the medical course of treatment usually proceeds in these cases.

Whiplash and soft tissue injuries

With many types of personal injury cases, we have to fight against insurance company propaganda and negative public perceptions that have developed over the last 20 or 30 years. Whiplash cases are a good example of this.

Whiplash—which is damage to the ligaments, the muscles, and/or the nerves in the neck or back—is the most common injury we see, especially in car accidents. What makes whiplash cases difficult is that you often can't see the injury. It's not like a fracture, which can be seen on an X-ray.

The good news is that there are now some newer, fairly sophisticated imaging techniques that can help to diagnose these injuries properly.

Just a little basic anatomy of the spine: The vertebrae are bones. Ligaments are the elastic tissue, kind of like rubber bands, that hold the vertebrae in place. In between the vertebrae are discs which act as shock absorbers. Running from the discs out through a hole in the vertebrae called the foramina are nerves. The nerves run down your arms, in the case of the neck, or cervical spine, and down your legs, in case of the lumbar spine (low back). You can't see the nerves or ligaments on a regular X-ray. If you have a whiplash or a soft tissue or a flexion-extension injury—various names for the same sort of thing—the ligaments can become damaged, but you can't see the damage on an X-ray.

Some newer types of diagnostic tools, like the digital motion X-ray or the flexion-extension MRI, can help to provide evidence of a whiplash or soft tissue injury. They offer a better look at how the anatomy moves, and you can extrapolate from there as to whether damage has been done to the ligaments. Without trying to get too technical, these tests show whether the vertebrae are moving more than would normally be expected when you move your neck. If the vertebrae aren't lining up properly, that can indicate a ligament tear.

This is important because the ligaments do not recover when they are damaged. They're not as vascularized, meaning the blood flow isn't great to them. A damaged ligament is sort of like a rubber band when it loses its stretch or gets worn out. At that point, the vertebral bodies aren't going to move the right way, and you could have too much motion. That can lead to stretching and injury in the nerves as well. It's also possible to have direct stretch injuries to the nerves as a result of the impact.

Soft tissue injuries can also occur in the lower back, or lumbar spine, and throughout the spine a herniated disc often compresses a nerve and produces pain. We often see various kinds of disc problems, such as a herniated or bulging disc.

The typical medical treatment in soft tissue injury cases starts conservatively, often with a chiropractor or a clinician who will refer you to physical therapy (PT). If you don't get better with PT, they will usually refer you to a radiologist for an MRI. If the MRI comes back positive (usually with a herniated disc), then you will be referred to a neurosurgeon or an orthopedic surgeon.

If right from the start you have significant neurological symptoms, such as radiating pain going down your arm or going down your leg, that normal treatment can be short-circuited, and they'll order an MRI immediately. A treating physician also might order steroids to reduce inflammation, which takes pressure off the nerves. There are numerous other spinal conditions such as facet joint arthritis that can be caused or aggravated by trauma which are amenable to injections, pain management, or other treatments as ordered by the appropriate physician.

What we as lawyers do in these soft tissue injury cases is refer the client to a treating physician. We let the client know that it's not an easy fix, and that despite the public perception, these injuries can be really painful. They can linger. They can be, and often are, permanent. It's just a difficult medical condition, and as a patient, you have to be on top of this situation. You have to consult back with your lawyer each step of the way. Of course, as lawyers, we have to caution the clients that we don't practice medicine. Every lawyer likes to envision himself as an amateur doctor, but we don't give medical advice.

We can give the benefit of the limited amount of knowledge we have to the client, because we've seen a lot of these cases through the years and have an idea as to what should happen.

If the symptoms are increasing dramatically, you need to get to an emergency room, but that's rare. Most of the time, the client is in treatment, we give them advice, and it progresses from conservative treatment to further diagnostic procedures if necessary. Treatment can involve shots, it can involve prescription steroids; it can involve traction; it can involve nerve blocks. There are a lot of different things that the doctors can recommend, and we as lawyers have to be somewhat familiar with all of those.

Points to Remember

1. Usually neck, back, and shoulders

2. Injuries can be hard to "see" so special radiological or diagnostic procedures are helpful.

3. A medical or chiropractic doctor who specializes in these injuries is a necessity.

Fractures/Nerve damage/Surgical cases

A significant number of our cases involve fractures and/or nerve damage. The fractures can range from simple broken bones fixed with a cast to complicated injuries requiring open reduction with internal fixation (surgery with plates and screws). Nerve damage can be a result of the original injury or a surgical complication. The defendant is liable for all injuries of this kind.

Any case in which there is a fracture or demonstrable nerve damage has significant value. The attorney should obtain the actual disc of the radiographic procedure (x-ray or

MRI) and consider having custom illustrations made by a professional medical illustrator. The family of the plaintiff should document his/her course of treatment with photos or videos. If the damages are severe a life care planner or economist can be retained to quantify the damages.

When there is a fracture or demonstrable nerve damage, the defendant and their insurance carrier are put on the defensive. It is more difficult for them to argue the injury is preexisting or simply does not exist. Juries award large sums in surgical cases because it is easy for them to understand the damages and the medical bills are significant.

It is very important in these cases to give the defense no easy openings to attack. Follow the doctor's orders. Do not miss appointments. Confer with your attorney if there is a problem with your medical treatment. We want the treating physician to be your friend, not your enemy. One word of warning: there is a natural human tendency to want to please your doctor. Along with this, there is a natural tendency to endure a certain amount of pain without complaint. Do not be too "macho" and fail to complain to the doctor or try to resume inadvisable activities. If it hurts, or there is weakness, tell your physician so there can be a note made in your medical record. If you are released from care, and over time pain develops or persists, go back to your doctor so there is a record. Remember, your lawyer has to prove permanent injury, and a jury can say, even in a case involving surgery, that the plaintiff has not been permanently injured.

Points to Remember

1. Sometimes not immediately diagnosed.
2. Cases are more valuable with objective evidence of injury.

3. Custom illustrations can be helpful; photos documenting medical treatment are very important.

4. Experts such as life care planners, and economists can quantify impact.

5. Defendant responsible for deficient medical care or subsequent injury.

6. Don't be "macho."

Spinal cord injuries: paraplegia or quadriplegia

Severe spinal injuries, or those involving paraplegia or quadriplegia, are exceptional cases with a whole different set of variables and considerations. First, any spinal cord injury is potentially life-threatening. Those who survive such an injury often suffer permanent consequences, and pursuing a case on their behalf can involve a much wider range of experts than the average personal injury case. In addition to accident reconstruction engineers and treating physicians, these experts might include economists, vocational experts, neurologists, neurosurgeons, radiologists, neuro-psychologists, psychiatrists, physical and occupational therapists, and life care planners. A catastrophic injury might require special needs trusts to help preserve government benefits. Your personal injury lawyer can help with all those considerations. Hire a lawyer who has experience with cases of this type. Patience and understanding the physical, psychological, and financial stresses and strains these catastrophic injuries place on the family is critical.

Given the catastrophic and life changing nature of these injuries, many hospitals have clinical social workers to help the family apply for government benefits or otherwise cope with an injury. Their help is invaluable. It is vitally important to follow up acute care with a top rehabilitation hospital.

Points to Remember

1. Hire an experienced lawyer who has handled catastrophic cases.

2. Use the hospital social worker as a resource.

3. Work to obtain admission to the best rehabilitation hospital.

4. Develop a life care plan.

Brain injury

Brain injuries are delicate and complex. Sometimes the injury is immediately obvious, but in other cases it is not. That's not as surprising as it might seem. In an emergency room, of course the doctors focus immediately on the most life-threatening injuries.

In an ER, the typical screening test for a suspected head injury is a CT scan, and if the CT scan is negative, they rule out a head injury, although they sometimes diagnose a concussion, which is a mild traumatic brain injury. Remember, the emergency rooms are screening for life-threatening injuries. In many cases the CT of the brain is negative.

In a recent case it wasn't until a follow-up appointment after discharge from the hospital that a client told his wife and his primary care physician, "You know, I haven't quite been the same. I've been dizzy. I've been having headaches; I'm sensitive to light. I can't always find the right words." Those are all typical symptoms in what is called a mild traumatic brain injury, if you can indeed say that any brain injury is mild.

In a mild traumatic brain injury case like this, it becomes the attorney's job to gather the experts together and present a convincing picture as to how the brain could be injured and the extent and scope of the injury.

If you go to your primary care physician and you say, "I have headaches, I have dizziness, I'm sensitive to light, I can't find the right words," a primary care physician who is on the ball will send you to see a neurologist or a neuropsychologist. They'll take a history and do a series of written tests to try and assess brain function.

The attorney in a case where there's a mild traumatic brain injury has to document the extent of the brain injury. Friends and family are often really important witnesses in a brain injury case, because they're the ones who can talk about what the client was like before and what they are like after. What has happened to them? What is the long-term effect?

Most people recover from a concussion-type injury, a mild traumatic brain injury, within a year or so. Some people do experience long-term effects. This is not something that is easily treatable.

Multiple experts are needed to document damages

It's the attorney's job to explain, document, and prove the injury as best he can. Before and after witnesses are important, along with neuropsychologists, neurologists, and physiatrists. If the injury is more serious and likely to be lasting, we hire a life care planner to talk about what treatment and therapy will be necessary. It might be counseling on how to cope with the injury. It might be the need of an aide. It might be hospitalization in a nursing home or rehabilitation center. It might even be a need for round-the-clock, 24/7 care. It is the job of a life care planner, who often is a medical doctor, to do the planning and come up with a number that the lawyer can present to a jury. Past and future medical expenses are part of the damages. We may also need an economist, because the expenses have to be brought down to present day value, and that's a very technical calculation. Other damages may be lost wages, lost benefits, and the loss of abilities to do things around the house. For instance, a spouse who used to care for the children and do the laundry can't do those things anymore. How do you quantify that? Only through an expert.

We may need a vocational expert to talk about what kind of jobs the injured person can do and can't do. So along with being sensitive to the stresses these situations put on the victim and the family, the lawyer has to be familiar with all these various aspects of dealing with the aftermath of brain injury. I want to get to know the client and their spouse. I want to talk to the children because they can often be valuable witnesses and help in counseling the individual as we go.

In terms of selecting an attorney, you want someone who will hire the right experts, who has some degree of knowledge, who will take your case seriously, and who will put the effort needed to get the best result possible. This is a lifelong injury. You have one shot at your day in court and you want to be sure that your attorney has done everything possible.

Frivolous defense experts

We've mentioned this issue before, and it certainly applies in brain injury cases as well. In dealing with insurance companies, you're dealing with an adversarial system. Suppose you are in an accident. You may have orthopedic injuries that can be easily proved, but if you say there's a brain injury, and it wasn't diagnosed immediately by the doctors, that's something the defense will fixate upon. They will hire an expert. In a recent brain injury case, the defense did hire an expert, a neuropsychologist. In her deposition, she claimed that if there was no one on the scene documenting that the victim had an alteration of consciousness—that the person was dizzy, or woozy, or just not quite right—then as an expert, she couldn't say that there was a brain injury. That's absolutely ridiculous. She also made the claim that mild traumatic brain injuries, by definition, cannot be permanent.

I pointed out that the very article she was citing as the basis for her opinion said that up to 20 percent of brain injuries are permanent. And her response was, "That's a myth. That's an urban myth." Then she contradicted herself when she was discussing the neurophysiological testing she had done on our client. She said, "Oh, I diagnosed it as depression, not an organic brain injury. Depression can be fixed and organic brain injury cannot really be fixed." You can see how frustrating it can be to deal with some of these so-called experts. In spite of all the defense efforts we usually achieve satisfactory results in our brain injury cases.

Miracles can happen

I've dealt with a number of brain injury cases over the years, but one in particular stands out. The young woman who suffered the injury—I'll call her Sarah—was a friend of our family. She and her boyfriend got into a bad car accident that left Sarah with a traumatic brain injury.

Sarah was in a coma, on life support, for weeks. At one point there was even a discussion about taking her off life support, but the decision was made not to remove the life support. Within two or three weeks of that decision being made, Sarah gradually began to wake up from her coma. When you're around brain injury cases, you learn that there are certain types of physicians and treatment facilities that are critically important, and here in Gainesville we are fortunate to have a great facility called Shands Rehabilitation Hospital. After Sarah began to wake up from her coma, she was transferred to Shands, where we visited her.

When you wake up from a coma, progress is very, very slow. Every case is different, but it's like the person is in a fog. They often can't talk, they can't function for themselves, and it takes a team to help them. It was highly gratifying to see the team of physical therapists, occupational therapists, speech therapists, and physical medicine physicians that came together at this facility to help Sarah. In this case there was limited coverage from an insurance policy. We did manage to negotiate a settlement that was in excess of the insurance policy; for years afterward the young man who was Sarah's former boyfriend made monthly payments for her because the insurance money just wasn't enough.

What I did as the attorney in her case was not as much traditional legal representation. One of the ways in which I practice law is collaboration. I talk to my partners and get ideas from them. I talk to other lawyers and get ideas from them. I also talk to treating professionals in various fields.

As a result of my having some back problems and surgeries, I had been referred to a tremendously skilled neuromuscular therapist named Randy Brower. Randy was someone who had an almost miraculous ability as a massage therapist; he was just extremely skilled with his hands and his fingers. Randy had an exercise physiologist he worked with named Greg Young.

Brain injury patients really need physical and mental stimulation. The more training and rehab that an individual gets after a brain injury, the better chance they have of some recovery. So I told Randy about Sarah and asked if he would be willing to take a look at her. For the next four to six years, Randy, at no charge, and Greg, at no charge, worked with Sarah at least twice a week, providing as much stimulation as possible to try and help Sarah recover as much as she could. I'm pleased to report now that Sarah got to the point where she was very functional. She has a limp when she walks and a slight slur to her speech. But she is now happily married to a great husband and she has two young children who are making A's in school. She's very happy. That's an example of a success story that is just highly gratifying to the lawyer. It's an example of what a lawyer can do for a client, aside from legal representation in court.

Since Sarah, I've represented a number of individuals who've suffered from a traumatic brain injury. Some of them were luckier than Sarah, in the sense that there were large insurance policies, so I've been able to make million dollar recoveries for them. But none of them are as lucky as Sarah in terms of having fantastic family support, and being able to go on to build a new life with her own young family. It's truly an amazing story.

Points to Remember

1. Every brain injury is significant.

2. An experienced lawyer is a necessity.

3. A rehabilitation hospital is critical to a patient's recovery.

4. Numerous experts need to be retained.

5. Good before and after witnesses are helpful.

Chapter 17: The Closing Statement

IN THIS BOOK, I've shared stories from every stage of my legal career, and it has been gratifying to look back over the past 40 years. I have really enjoyed the practice of law. I've never been bored. I've always been intellectually challenged. Sometimes I've been really disappointed; sometimes I've been exhilarated, but I've never been bored.

I really enjoy helping people. As we're talking right now, one of my clients, a young mother with a six-month-old baby, is walking in the door. It will be my pleasure to sit down with her, sign a couple documents, and hand her a check for a significant amount of money, which is fair compensation for her recently concluded case. I enjoy doing that; it's one of the best parts of my day. I enjoy counseling people and helping people. I enjoy appearing in court. I think that having an attorney who enjoys what he's doing and sees its intrinsic worth has benefited my clients over the years. That may be one more piece of advice for someone who is looking for an attorney: Find an attorney who is not only committed to your case, but who also loves the work that he or she does on your behalf.

When I started out in private practice, as I related earlier, I had two partners who followed me from the criminal law side of things. We had all come from the public defender's office, and eventually shifted our practice into civil law with a focus on personal injury.

My original partners, Tom Farkash and Alan Parlapiano, have both retired. Now our firm has become something of a family affair: I have the privilege of practicing with my wife, Cherie Fine, and my daughter, Julie Fine. Today our firm includes six attorneys, all Gator alumni. We are able to offer our clients more than 100 years of combined legal experience.

A family affair

Our motto as a firm is: "When life changes, we're there." That's always been our commitment to our clients and it remains so today. This is why I think we've been successful as a law firm: We try to do the right thing for our clients, and we're experienced enough to know what the right thing is.

I think one thing that differentiates us from other law firms is our willingness to litigate cases if necessary. Many firms that do this kind of work, based on my observations, are not really willing to litigate cases. When you hire a lawyer, you need to ask specifically what they do with a case that needs to go into litigation. Unfortunately many lawyers lack the skill, the resources, and the motivation to pursue the case to a jury trial or to an appeal.

Maybe it comes from having spent so much time in the criminal justice system. As young lawyers our early careers compelled us to be in court every day. We all became very comfortable in the courtroom, and that probably made us more willing to litigate when needed.

When my wife Cherie came on board, she also switched from doing criminal defense work to civil plaintiffs' work, so she'd had that same experience of being in court consistently.

Unlike me, Cherie grew up in the legal system, in De-Land, Florida. Her stepfather was an attorney; her mom had been his legal secretary. Cherie's stepfather was eventually named a judge, and served very successfully as a circuit judge in Volusia County for many years. So from a very young age, Cherie was indoctrinated into the legal system.

That upbringing, I think, gave her a really good understanding of what it takes to be successful and how hard work is rewarded with good results in the legal system. She also grew up with a commitment to giving back and serving the community; she has carried that throughout her life. She's on the board of the University of Florida and on the board of the Humane Society. She was an officer in the Junior League. Next year she's going to be the bar president; right now she's chair of the grievance committee.

Our daughter Julie joined us in 2016, after four years in the state attorney's office.

I was very pleased when Julie decided to go to law school. She had been a music major, and I think my wife would have been very happy for Julie to play the cello in an orchestra somewhere. Julie was a highly skilled classical musician, and her dedication and focus learned in her music studies has translated very well to her career as a skilled trial lawyer.

When Julie was graduating law school, her clinic teacher was the Chief Assistant State Attorney. The teacher called Cherie and me and told us that she really wanted to recruit Julie for the State Attorney's Office. Well, her mother and I reacted very differently. Cherie thought that Julie should come and work with us. I thought Julie would benefit from going to the State Attorney's Office and gaining the same kind of experience I had gained in the public defender's office. That experience brought me to the point where being in court is as comfortable and natural as being in my living room. That's what I wanted for Julie.

I urged both Cherie and Julie to follow my advice. I set up a series of conferences with various trial lawyers and judges and put the question to them. Frankly, it was no contest. I knew what they would say, and they all said go do the state attorney job. So Julie took the state attorney job, she got comfortable in the courtroom, and then she joined us.

With all the litigation and investigation experience she had acquired as an assistant state attorney, Julie hit the ground running. In 2017, the National Trial Lawyers Association named her one of their top 40 under 40 trial lawyers. We're proud to have her practicing with us.

As a firm, we believe very much in giving back to our profession and to our community. Along with all of Cherie's other commitments, she has taught legal research and writing at the University of Florida College of Law. I've been teaching trial practice at the law school for the last 25 years or so, and I've brought both Cherie and Julie with me. Last year, I taught the class with Julie, and it was a lot of fun, even when our philosophical disagreements played out in front of our law students. We've enjoyed it very much, and it's our pleasure to help law students learn how to do trial work which is not taught in Socratic law school classes.

Over the years, members of our firm have been involved in a number of charitable and community activities throughout Gainesville and the greater North Florida Area, with a particular focus on educational and environmental programs. We take great pride in our Gainesville community.

The next generation: A word from Julie Fine

Julie Fine: How did I get here? It's probably because of how I was raised. As I was growing up, at the dinner table with my family, my dad was always asking us questions: How do you feel about this? What do you think about this? Let me give you a fact pattern. And we would be discussing it or arguing about it. That's really where it all started.

I was actually a music major, and as my dad mentioned, my mother wanted me to stay with music for as long as possible, but I just really loved being able to figure stuff out and solve problems. Even in studying for the LSAT, I really loved when we had to problem solve or come up with the facts and fit them to a situation. Coming from music school, which was extremely demanding, I found law school to be fun. I loved it and I found it really interesting.

I got to intern at the state attorney's office while I was in law school and even had the chance to do a trial, a UI trial. And I won, so of course that was fun.

After I finished law school and passed the bar, the state attorney's office offered me a job. I wasn't expecting that; I was training to come and work at my parents' firm. But I did go to the state attorney's office for several years, where I gained a lot of trial experience.

I worked in traffic, which I think blended well with my upbringing. I felt that drunk drivers were the kind of individuals for whom the crime itself is a deterrent. I understand that there is alcoholism and other issues, but often it's just people making bad decisions. I think that if people know that they're going to get in trouble, that they're going to be prosecuted, and this is going to cause them a lot of harm, they're more likely to not do it. To me, prosecuting DUIs was a good thing in our college town. I was not willing to cut breaks for kids who maybe had more money than others. I think that's how I developed a bit of a reputation. The defense attorneys and public defenders started calling me the Prosecutrix. I found it rather flattering, honestly.

I also used to set a large number of cases for trial. We had a backlog of old cases and I thought it was ridiculous and unfair that these people had to sit around and wait. So I would just set them for trial. Most of them plead out, and usually you end up with only one or two. But one week, I had three cases set for trial, all DUIs. I wanted to do jury selection, so I had to do the first two in the morning. Then, a judge let me skip out and run back behind the courthouse to run into the other courtroom to do the third jury selection. I was able to do all three trials and I won all three. I think I still have the record for winning the most trials in a week in the Eighth Judicial Circuit.

During my time at the state attorney's office, I also received an award from Mothers Against Drunk Driving, Northeast Florida. It was recognition for my prosecuting DUI cases. It was an honor to receive the plaque, but I was even more pleased because you had to be nominated by local law enforcement to receive that award. I didn't know they were going to do that, and it was really important to me to know that law enforcement thought I was doing a good job. I was proud of that.

After I left the state attorney's office in 2015, I eventually made my way back here to civil practice with my parents. I think we all thought that would happen eventually. My parents were trying a lot more cases. They needed another hand on deck, and my time as a prosecutor actually prepared me well to move into working as a plaintiff's attorney.

Being a prosecutor and being a plaintiff's attorney are somewhat the same, because we're the ones with the burden. We're putting on the case; we're prosecuting the individual who has maybe done something wrong. We have to prove it. That's our role.

As a prosecutor, you have to collect all the evidence. You have to organize it. You have to figure out what actually happened—what the truth is. You have to determine the most effective and efficient way to present that truth to someone to help them see exactly what you're seeing. I might be able to figure it out over a period of months, but then it has to be condensed into a few days or even just a few hours for jurors. That's the hard part, especially when you have the other side working against you and sometimes it feels like they're just making things up. Don't get me wrong; I think there are some really great defense attorneys who are good people. And I also think a lot of the other side's job is to try to make our job as difficult as possible.

I think, for a defense attorney, that's more than fair. A prosecutor should have to prove guilt beyond a reasonable doubt. We should have to have the evidence to support it. Whatever legal means that the defense attorney can find—whether the prosecutor's not prepared, or doesn't have the information—is more than fair. I bring that same belief into my civil practice, even though the burden of proof is different. As plaintiffs' attorneys we need to be as prepared as possible and have all the information.

We also have to believe in our clients. It's really rewarding to be able to stand up for someone who's been hurt or wronged, and isn't being treated fairly, and then to prove that they were right, and help them recover some compensation.

I see how frustrating these situations are for our clients. They've been put in a horrible position with their injuries and often feel as if there's nothing they can do. It's like when you're sick for a few days, and you say, "Oh, I'd do anything to feel better. This cold, this sinus infection, I would do anything to make it go away." That's how our clients feel about their injuries. They'd do anything to make them go away, but they can't. That, to me, is heartbreaking. It's adding insult to injury when the defense goes after our clients who have been hurt, and then insults them by calling them liars.

I get really upset for our clients. I can't imagine dealing with what they are going through. If it were to happen to me, I would hope to have someone just as upset as I am working for me.

I grew up with parents who were always helping people who had been hurt, sometimes catastrophically hurt. Being around that is hard, but I saw how good it is to be able to help people who need help. If you can do that and find your job interesting at the same time, that's a great combination.

After I finished law school, I started helping my dad with trial practice at the University of Florida Law School. I coach with him. It's really fun, because he's the opposite of me in terms of his skills. He's a great cross-examiner; he sees the big picture very easily. I, on the other hand, am detail-oriented and I am a direct examiner. His background was criminal defense, and mine is prosecution, so it's almost a yin and yang, which I think is really good for the students. I also think they liked having someone there who was younger to help them because I was actually trying cases every month, one or two trials a month. So I knew exactly what was going on, especially in our circuit, and could offer that practical experience.

When I joined my parents in their practice in 2016, I had to learn how to adapt to each of their styles. They're both amazing, exceptional people, but they're very different in the way they work. In a way, they're opposites.

My mom is a Renaissance woman. She does everything. She's a lawyer. She's an amazing chef. She's a gardener. She has chickens. She has bees. She serves on multiple boards in the community. She does all of these things along with being a full-time lawyer and being a mom. I don't know how she does it!

It was a bit of a challenge for my mom and me when we first started trying cases, just getting in the flow of who does what. Because while my father is very good at collaborating, and speaking, and communicating with me, my mother is trying to get every single thing done herself, and doesn't always tell me what she's doing. I try cases with both of them, so I had to figure it out: Okay, this is how she works. This is how he works. It just happens to be opposite.

But I started getting the hang of it pretty quickly. My mother and I won all three of our cases that fall of 2016, and they were very big wins, on soft tissue injuries. People may think of those as not a big deal, but it's a big deal to a client who had to have shoulder surgery and couldn't hold her newborn when she gave birth.

It was good to get the hang of things with my mom, to learn her brain, and see how she likes things done. I think we've become a great team. My dad and I are still working really hard as well. His recent cases have been large, catastrophic injuries, and those take so much work. So I'm always working, but I love it.

Jack's Closing Statement: Maximizing the Case

I have already discussed many of the factors involved in maximizing your personal injury settlement. Don't make early mistakes at the scene, get medically evaluated, and hire a good, experienced lawyer who will communicate with you. We have also discussed the normal way a case proceeds in terms of treatment, a doctor signing off on permanent injury, and a demand to the insurance carrier. What frequently comes next is a substandard, bad faith offer from the defendant's carrier. So how do we maximize the offer, aside from the typical back-and-forth negotiating?

Litigation is the answer. Filing a lawsuit often results, after much additional hard work and time, in a doubling, tripling or quadrupling of the offer. I have enclosed some presuit offers and post-suit settlements as Exhibit E in the Appendix. These documents prove that being aggressive works. Why does it work?

The insurance companies are not stupid. They know that if a competent attorney files a lawsuit, they are in for a fight. There are costs they must expend to pay their own attorneys (particularly if they hire a private law firm) and for experts, as well as deposition transcripts and other expenses. There is a risk of losing big time if a jury does not like their arguments. A Proposal for Settlement can put extra pressure on the insurance company, subjecting them to attorney's fees for plaintiff's counsel. The Proposal for Settlement uses the greed of the insurance companies against them. Overall, our experience with litigation has been overwhelmingly positive.

It is critically important to scrutinize those cases going into litigation. Not every case is suitable. Generally, you should look at the factors we discussed earlier regarding liability, impact, objective evidence of injury, etc. If the case has several weaknesses in those areas, it may not be a good candidate for litigation. If there is no real weakness, then by all means, we would recommend initiating the suit. Of course, the decision is up to the client.

A word of warning: litigation is uncertain. Juries cannot always be predicted. However, most cases that are filed do settle, either at mediation or shortly after mediation. When a case is in litigation, the value can go up or down depending on factors inherent in the litigation process. For example, if the plaintiff's treating physician does not back up statements he made in the records, the case gets weaker. If the treating physician gives a good deposition, the case gets stronger. The development of witness testimony, documentary evidence, and trial strategy, all affect the value of a case. Communication directly with the trial lawyer concerning the progress of the case is always helpful. Together you will make the right decision.

Into the future

In our modern world, it often seems that bigger institutional corporate interests are squeezing the individual, trying to deprive the individual of their rights and of justice. That's what we work against: We're sticking up for the little guy. As plaintiffs' personal injury lawyers, we're able to represent the average citizen against corporate interests. I believe there's something very worthwhile in doing that. We've been doing it for a long time, and we look forward to doing that for many years to come.

Appendix

Seven Common Mistakes to Avoid After an Auto Accident

1. Failure to call police: This is a mistake because the police accident report, although not admissible in a personal injury lawsuit, can be very helpful. A police conclusion of fault is persuasive with the insurance company. Furthermore, Florida law requires notification of the police in most crash situations.

2. Failure to get medically evaluated: Obviously, if there is any question of a medical injury, medical evaluation should be immediate. Sometimes an individual will think he or she is fine, then be sore the next day and try to "tough it out." Please be aware of the 14-day provision which excludes PIP benefits if you have not been evaluated by a physician. See a doctor if there is any question of an injury.

3. Failure to acknowledge prior medical history: Insurance companies always try to cast doubt on the credibility of the victim. Do not give them ammunition by making mis-statements regarding past medical conditions. Be sure to mention to any treating physician all prior injuries or conditions involving your affected body part if they ask. Sometimes it is hard to remember, but do your best.

4. Failure to take photos or document the evidence: Everyone has access to a phone with a camera. After a crash, take photos of the property damage from close up and farther away. If you have a ruler or tape measure include that in the photos. Take photos of the scene from several different angles. Scrutinize the area for any nearby businesses that may have video cameras.

5. Failure to control social media: If you are hurt, do not push yourself. You should be especially careful of pushing yourself and putting your activities on social media. The defense will obtain your social media posts, photos, etc. and will try to use this information to weaken your case.

6. Failure to hire an attorney: I admit it, I have a bias here. However, long experience has proven that insurance companies will try to take advantage of an unrepresented claimant. Try to hire an experienced, aggressive attorney who has actually taken your kind of accident case to trial.

7. Failure to follow through: This mistake can relate to hiring an attorney, communicating with the attorney, continuing with medical treatment, or just filling out required paperwork. See the doctor for follow-ups; do not be a "no show" for appointments without calling. Ask your attorney any questions that occur to you.

EXHIBIT A
SAMPLE ADMINISTRATIVE FORM
AUTHORITY TO REPRESENT AND
CONTINGENCY FEE AGREEMENT

I, the undersigned client, do hereby retain and employ the Law Firm of _____ as my attorney(s) to represent me in my claim for damages against _____ or any other party, firm or corporation liable therefore, resulting from an accident that occurred on _____.

I HEREBY AGREE to pay for the costs incurred by _____ in prosecuting this claim and authorize them to undertake and/or incur such costs as they may deem necessary from time to time. These costs include, but are not limited to, such items as police reports, hospital and medical records, photographs, filing fee, costs of serving summonses and subpoenas, court reporter fees, jury list, exhibits, state records, investigation expenses, and expert witness fees, including fees for medical testimony and fees for medical conferences. They will make every effort to keep these costs at an absolute minimum consistent with the requirements of the case. At the time the case is closed, an accounting will be made for all disbursements made in my case.

As compensation for their services, I agree to pay my said attorney(s) from the proceeds of recovery the following fee:

a. Before the filing of an answer or the demand for appointment of arbitrators or, if no answer is filed or no demand for appointment of arbitrators is made, the expiration of the time period provided for such action:

1. 33-1/3% of any recovery up to $1 million; plus
2. 30% of any portion of the recovery between $1 million and $2 million; plus
3. 20% of any portion of the recovery exceeding $2 million.

b. After the filing of an answer or the demand for appointment of arbitrators or, if no answer is filed or no demand for appointment of arbitrators is made, the expiration of the time period provided for such action, through the entry of judgment:

1. 40% of any recovery up to $1 million; plus
2. 30% of any portion of the recovery between $1 million and $2 million; plus
3. 20% of any portion of the recovery exceeding $2 million.

c. If all defendants admit liability at the time of filing their answers and request a trial only on damages:

1. 33-1/3% of any recovery up to $1 million; plus
2. 20% of any portion of the recovery between $1 million and $2 million; plus
3. 15% of any portion of the recovery exceeding $2 million.

d. An additional 5% of any recovery after institution of any appellate proceeding is filed or post judgment relief or action is required for recovery on the judgment.

IT IS AGREED and UNDERSTOOD that this employment is upon a contingent fee basis, and if no recovery is made, I will not be indebted to my attorneys for any sum whatsoever as attorney's fees.

THE UNDERSIGNED CLIENT HAS, BEFORE SIGN-ING THIS CONTRACT, RECEIVED AND READ THE STATEMENT OF CLIENT'S RIGHTS, AND UNDER-STANDS EACH OF THE RIGHTS SET FORTH THERE-IN. THE UNDERSIGNED CLIENT HAS SIGNED THE STATEMENT AND RECEIVED A SIGNED COPY TO KEEP TO REFER TO WHILE BEING REPRESENTED BY THE UNDERSIGNED ATTORNEY(S).

THIS CONTRACT MAY BE CANCELLED BY WRITTEN NOTIFICATION TO THE ATTORNEY AT ANY TIME WITHIN 3 BUSINESS DAYS OF THE DATE THE CONTRACT WAS SIGNED, AS SHOWN BELOW, AND IF CANCELLED THE CLIENT SHALL NOT BE OBLIGATED TO PAY ANY FEES TO THE ATTORNEY(S) FOR THE WORK PERFORMED DURING THAT TIME. IF THE ATTORNEY(S) HAVE ADVANCED FUNDS TO OTHERS IN REPRESENTATION OF THE CLIENT, THE ATTORNEY(S) ARE ENTITLED TO BE REIMBURSED FOR SUCH AMOUNTS AS THEY HAVE REASONABLY ADVANCED ON BEHALF OF THE CLIENT.

DATED THIS _____ day of _____, 20____.

_____   _____
[Client's Printed Name]   [Client's Signature]

The above employment is hereby accepted upon the terms stated above.

DATED THIS _____ day of _____, 20____.

_____   _____
[Attorney's Printed Name]   [Attorney's Signature]

EXHIBIT B
SAMPLE ADMINISTRATIVE FORM
STATEMENT OF CLIENT'S RIGHTS FOR
CONTINGENCY FEES

Before you, the prospective client, arrange a contingent fee agreement with a lawyer, you should understand this statement of your rights as a client. This statement is not a part of the actual contract between you and your lawyer, but, as a prospective client, you should be aware of these rights:

1. There is no legal requirement that a lawyer charge a client a set fee or a percentage of money recovered in a case. You, the client, have the right to talk with your lawyer about the proposed fee and to bargain about the rate or percentage as in any other contract. If you do not reach an agreement with 1 lawyer you may talk with other lawyers.

2. Any contingent fee contract must be in writing and you have 3 business days to reconsider the contract. You may cancel the contract without any reason if you notify your lawyer in writing within 3 business days of signing the contract. If you withdraw from the contract within the first 3 business days, you do not owe the lawyer a fee although you may be responsible for the lawyer's actual costs during that time. If your lawyer begins to represent you, your lawyer may not withdraw from the case without giving you notice, delivering necessary papers to you, and allowing you time to employ another lawyer. Often, your lawyer must obtain court approval before withdrawing from a case. If you discharge your lawyer without good cause after the 3-day period, you may have to pay a fee for work the lawyer has done. (RRTFB* April 30, 2018)

3. Before hiring a lawyer, you, the client, have the right to know about the lawyer's education, training, and experience. If you ask, the lawyer should tell you specifically about the lawyer's actual experience dealing with cases similar to yours. If you ask, the lawyer should provide information about special training or knowledge and give you this information in writing if you request it.

4. Before signing a contingent fee contract with you, a lawyer must advise you whether the lawyer intends to handle your case alone or whether other lawyers will be helping with the case. If your lawyer intends to refer the case to other lawyers, the lawyer should tell you what kind of fee sharing arrangement will be made with the other lawyers. If lawyers from different law firms will represent you, at least 1 lawyer from each law firm must sign the contingent fee contract.

5. If your lawyer intends to refer your case to another lawyer or counsel with other lawyers, your lawyer should tell you about that at the beginning. If your lawyer takes the case and later decides to refer it to another lawyer or to associate with other lawyers, you should sign a new contract that includes the new lawyers. You, the client, also have the right to consult with each lawyer working on your case and each lawyer is legally responsible to represent your interests and is legally responsible for the acts of the other lawyers involved in the case.

6. You, the client, have the right to know in advance how you will need to pay the expenses and the legal fees at the end of the case. If you pay a deposit in advance for costs, you may ask reasonable questions about how the money will be or has been spent and how much of it remains unspent.

Your lawyer should give a reasonable estimate about future necessary costs. If your lawyer agrees to lend or advance you money to prepare or research the case, you have the right to know periodically how much money your lawyer has spent on your behalf. You also have the right to decide, after consulting with your lawyer, how much money is to be spent to prepare a case. If you pay the expenses, you have the right to decide how much to spend. Your lawyer should also inform you whether the fee will be based on the gross amount recovered or on the amount recovered minus the costs.

7. You, the client, have the right to be told by your lawyer about possible adverse consequences if you lose the case. Those adverse consequences might include money that you might have to pay to your lawyer for costs and liability you might have for attorney's fees, costs, and expenses to the other side.

8. You, the client, have the right to receive and approve a closing statement at the end of the case before you pay any money. The statement must list all of the financial details of the entire case, including the amount recovered, all expenses, and a precise statement of your lawyer's fee. Until you approve the closing statement your lawyer cannot pay any money to anyone, including you, without an appropriate order of the court. You also have the right to have every lawyer or law firm working on your case sign this closing statement.

9. You, the client, have the right to ask your lawyer at reasonable intervals how the case is progressing and to have these questions answered to the best of your lawyer's ability. (RRTFB April 30, 2018)

10. You, the client, have the right to make the final decision regarding settlement of a case. Your lawyer must notify you of all offers of settlement before and after the trial. Offers during the trial must be immediately communicated and you should consult with your lawyer regarding whether to accept a settlement. However, you must make the final decision to accept or reject a settlement.

11. If at any time you, the client, believe that your lawyer has charged an excessive or illegal fee, you have the right to report the matter to The Florida Bar, the agency that oversees the practice and behavior of all lawyers in Florida. For information on how to reach The Florida Bar, call 850/561-5600, or contact the local bar association. Any disagreement between you and your lawyer about a fee can be taken to court and you may wish to hire another lawyer to help you resolve this disagreement. Usually fee disputes must be handled in a separate lawsuit, unless your fee contract provides for arbitration. You can request, but may not require, that a provision for arbitration (under Chapter 682, Florida Statutes, or under the fee arbitration rule of the Rules Regulating The Florida Bar) be included in your fee contract.

_____   _____
Client Signature   Date

_____   _____
Attorney Signature   Date

*RRTFB: Rules Regulating the Florida Bar

EXHIBIT C
IN THE CIRCUIT COURT OF THE EIGHTH
JUDICIAL CIRCUIT
IN AND FOR ALACHUA COUNTY, FLORIDA

JOHN DOE
 Plaintiff,
-vs-
JANE SMITH,
 Defendant.

CASE NO: 2018-CA-XXXX
DIVISION: K

DEFENDANT'S INTERROGATORIES
TO PLAINTIFF

1. What is the name, address, telephone number, date of birth, driver's license number and social security number of the person answering these interrogatories, and if applicable, the person's official position or relationship with the party to whom the interrogatories are directed?

2. List the names, business addresses, dates of employment and rates of pay regarding all employers, including self-employment, for whom you have worked in the past ten years.

3. List all former names and when you were known by those names. State all addresses where you have lived for the past ten years, the dates you lived at each address, and if you are or have ever been married, the name of your spouse or spouses.

4. Do you wear glasses, contact lenses, or hearing aids? If so, state who prescribed them; when they were prescribed; when your eyes or ears were last examined; and the name and address of the examiner?

5. Have you ever been convicted of a crime, other than any juvenile adjudication, which under the law under which you were convicted was punishable by death or imprisonment in excess of one year, or that involved dishonesty or a false statement regardless of the punishment? If so, state as to each conviction the specific crime, the date and the place of the conviction.

6. Were you suffering from physical infirmity, disability, or sickness at the time of the incident described in the Complaint? If so, what was the nature of the infirmity, disability, or sickness?

7. Did you consume any alcoholic beverages or take any drugs or medication within twelve hours before the time of the incident described in the Complaint? If so, state the type and amount of alcoholic beverages, drugs or medication which were consumed and when and where you consumed them.

8. Describe in detail how the incident described in the Complaint happened, including all actions taken by you to prevent the incident.

9. Describe in detail each act or omission on the part of any party to this lawsuit that you contend constituted negligence that was a contributing legal cause of the incident in question.

10. Were you charged with any violation of law (including any regulations or ordinances) arising out of the incident described in the Complaint? If so, please state the nature of the charge; what pleas, or answer, if any, you entered to the charge; what court or agency heard the charge; whether any written report was prepared by anyone regarding this charge, and if so, the name and address of the person or entity that prepared

the report; whether you have a copy of the report; and whether the testimony at any trial, hearing, or other proceeding on the charge was recorded in any manner, and, if so, the name and address of the person who recorded the testimony.

11. Describe each injury for which you are claiming damages in this case, specifying the part of your body that was injured, the nature of the injury, and, as to any injuries you contend are permanent, the effects on you that you claim are permanent.

12. List each item of expense or damage, other than loss of income or earning capacity, that you claim to have incurred as a result of the incident described in the Complaint, giving for each item the date incurred, the name and business address to whom each was paid or is owed, and the goods or services for which it was incurred. Include all medical bills and any other damages.

13. Do you contend that you have any income, benefits, or earning capacity in the past or future as a result of the incident described in the Complaint? If so, state the nature of the income, benefits, or earning capacity, and the amount and the method that you used in computing the amount.

14. Has anything been paid or is anything payable from any third party (including any PIP or Med Pay insurer) for the damages listed in your answers to these interrogatories? If so, state the amounts paid or payable, the name and business address of the person or entity who paid or owes said amounts, and which of those third parties have a claim or right of subrogation.

15. List the names and business addresses of each physician who has treated or examined you, and each medical facility

where you have received any treatment or examination for the injuries for which you seek damages in this case. State as to each physician the date of treatment or examination and the injury or condition for which you were examined or treated.

16. List the names and business addresses of all other physicians, medical facilities or other health care providers by whom or at which you have been examined or treated in the past ten years, and state as to each the dates of examination or treatment and the condition or injury for which you were examined or treated.

17. List the names and addresses of all persons who are believed or known by you, your agents or attorneys to have any knowledge concerning any of the issues in this lawsuit; and specify the subject matter about which the witness has knowledge.

18. Have you heard or do you know about any statement or remark made by or on behalf of any party to this lawsuit that in any way relates to this lawsuit? If so, state the name and address of each person who made the statement or statements, the name and address of each person who heard it , and the date, time, place and substance of each statement.

19. State the name and address of every person known to you, your agents, or attorneys, to have knowledge about, or possession, custody or control of any model, plat, map, drawing, motion picture, video tape, or photograph pertaining to any fact or issue involved in this controversy. As to each such person describe what such person has, the name and address of the person who took or prepared it, and the date it was taken or prepared.

20. Do you intend to call any expert witnesses at the trial of this case? If so, state as to each such witness the name and business address of the witness, the witness's qualifications as an expert, the subject matter upon which the witness is expected to testify, the substance of the facts and opinions to which the witness is expected to testify, and a summary of the grounds for each opinion.

21. Please state if you have ever been a party, a Plaintiff or Defendant, in a lawsuit other than the present matter and if so, state whether you were Plaintiff or Defendant, the nature of the action, and the date and court in which such suit was filed.

22. At the time of the incident described in the Complaint, were you wearing a seat belt? If not, please state why not; where you were seated in the vehicle; and whether the vehicle was equipped with a seat belt that was operational and available for your use.

23. Did any mechanical defect in the motor vehicle in which you were riding at the time of the incident described in the Complaint contribute to the incident? If so, describe the nature of the defect and how it contributed to the incident.

24. Have you belonged to or been a member of health clubs, gyms, athletic or fitness clubs or organizations within the past five (5) years? If so, state the name and address of each such facility and your dates of membership.

25. Please state the name and address of any health care provider from whom you have sought treatment for any psychological, psychiatric or emotional illness.

26. If the alleged injury or injuries sustained in the accident prevent you or make it more difficult for you to perform your

work or occupation or in any way inhibit you or interfere with your daily activities (including recreational activities), please state specifically in what manner you are affected.

27. Please list by name and address every entity, including without limitation medical providers, to whom you or your attorney has issued a letter of protection or lie in connection with this action.

28. Have you ever suffered any injuries in any event or any accident (this includes, but is not limited to, car accidents, slip and falls, or on the job injuries) either prior to or subsequent to the incident referred to in the Complaint? This request includes a disclosure of any similar complaints/injuries, whether it be from a traumatic event or not, prior to the accident alleged in the Complaint. If so, state:

   a. The date and place of such event or accident, that resulted in injury.
   b. A detailed description of all the injuries you received.
   c. The names and addresses of all health care providers and hospitals rendering treatment.
   d. The name and address of each and every attorney retained to represent you for a claim related to each accident.

29. Please state what radiographic films you have in your possession, or your attorneys' possession, listing the date of the film, type of film, area involved and the name and address of the facility the film was taken.

30. List the names and addresses of all locations where you have had prescriptions filled for the time period of five years before the accident up to and including the present time.

EXHIBIT D

AUTO POLICY DECLARATIONS

Summary

Named Insureds	**Your Agent:**	**Payment**
John Doe	Jane Smith	
123 Main St.	123-555-5555	
Anywhere, USA 12345		

POLICY NUMBER
111-222-33333333
(Your policy number may contain additional characters, and different numbers of digits)

EFFECTIVE PERIOD
1/1/20XX – 12/31/20XX 12:01 A.M. EST

Driver(s) Listed	**Driver(s) Excluded**
John Doe	None

Vehicles Covered	**VIN**	**Lienholder**
1. 2018 Go Mobile	XXX-123-ABCDE-1	XYZ Auto Financing

TOTAL PREMIUM

Premium for Go Mobile	$350
TOTAL	$350

SAMPLE COVERAGE FOR VEHICLE 1

POLICY NUMBER
111-222-33333333
(Your policy number may contain additional characters, and different numbers of digits)

Vehicle: 2018 Go Mobile

Coverage	Limits		Deductible	Premium
Auto Liability				
Bodily Injury	$100,000	Each person	N/A	$100
	$300,000	Each occurrence		
Property Damage	$100,000	Each occurrence	N/A	$50
Uninsured Motorist (Includes underinsured, nonstackable)	$100,000	Each person	N/A	$50
	$300,000	Each occurrence	N/A	
Auto Medical Payments	$5,000	Each Person	N/A	$75
Auto Collision Insurance	Cash value		$500	$150
Auto Comprehensive Insurance	Cash value		$500	$15
Rental Reimbursement	$35 per day		N/A	$10
			TOTAL	$350

DISCOUNTS

RATING INFO

EXHIBIT E

Pre-litigation Offers and Post-litigation Results

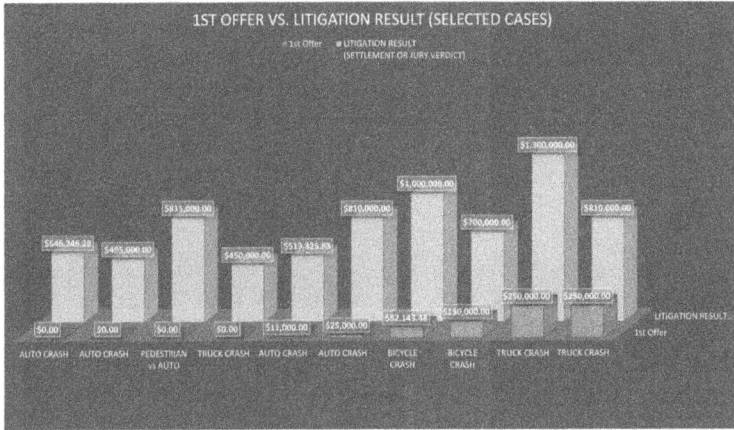

About the Author

Jack Fine was born in New York, New York and was raised in the northeast, where he studied sociology at Colby College in Waterville, Maine. He graduated with honors from the University of Florida Levin College of Law in 1976 and was admitted into the Florida Bar the same year.

Upon graduation, Mr. Fine practiced as an Assistant Public Defender in the Third Judicial Circuit office in Lake City from 1976-1977. He then worked as an Assistant Public Defender in the Gainesville office of the Public Defender from 1977-1980. In 1980, he founded the firm, which is now known as Fine, Farkash, & Parlapiano, P.A. where he wanted to exclusively represent victims of personal injury in claims against negligent parties.

Mr. Fine is a highly experienced personal injury attorney and is recognized for his commitment to the law. He coached a trial team for the University of Florida Levin College of Law in 1994 and has taught as an adjunct faculty in the trial practice course at the law school since 1983.